WELLSPRINGS

A Book of Spiritual Exercises

WELLSPRINGS
A Book of Spiritual Exercises

ANTHONY DE MELLO, S.J.

Complete and unabridged

AN IMAGE BOOK
DOUBLEDAY
NEW YORK LONDON TORONTO SYDNEY AUCKLAND

AN IMAGE BOOK
Published by DOUBLEDAY, a division of
Bantam Doubleday Dell Publishing Group, Inc.,
666 Fifth Avenue, New York, New York 10103.

IMAGE, DOUBLEDAY and the portrayal of a cross
intersecting a circle are trademarks of Doubleday, a
division of Bantam Doubleday Dell Publishing Group, Inc.

Originally published in India
by Gujarat Sahitya Prakash

This edition published by special arrangement
with Center for Spiritual Exchange.

Imprimi Potest: Edwin Rasquinha S.J.
                     Praep. Prov. Bomb.
                     November 11, 1983.

Imprimatur: ✠ C. Gomes S.J.
                     Bishop of Ahmedabad.
                     December 6, 1983.

Library of Congress Cataloging-in-Publication Data

De Mello, Anthony, 1931–
Wellsprings: a book of spiritual exercises.

"Complete and unabridged."
"Originally published in India by Gujarat Sahitya Prakash"—T.p.
verso.
1. Spiritual exercises.   I. Title.
[BX2182.2.D393   1986]   248.3   86–4478
ISBN 0-385-19617-2 (pbk.)

4   6   8   10   11   9   7   5

BG

To the Jesuit Order
that I feel so proud
and so unworthy
to belong to.

In spite of frequent references
to Jesus Christ, whose disciple the
author professes himself to be,
this book is meant for people
of all spiritual affiliations—
religious, areligious, agnostic,
atheistic.

CONTENTS

REALITY

RESTORATION

CHRIST

LIFE

LOVE

SILENCE

SEEDLINGS

These exercises have a power that will not be experienced if they are merely read. They must be done. This is true of almost every sentence in an exercise. Often what seems to be an uninspiring set of words when read may prove to be, surprisingly, a gateway to enlightenment when done.

If the exercises are practiced in a group, the leader reads one aloud with frequent pauses. . . . Each member of the group, however, must keep his or her own interior pace and not the leader's. In other words, feel free to stay behind while the leader reads ahead; even to ignore his or her words entirely, if you are gripped by something that appeals to you and bids you stay.

If you do the exercises alone it is best to read the exercise attentively, then put the book aside and do as much of it as you remember. Repeated reference to the book will prove distracting. You need not do an exercise in its entirety. You may choose to do a fragment either because you have no time for more or because the fragment offers so much fruit that you feel no inclination to move on to something else.

Do an exercise repeatedly, for in the repetition one sometimes gains access to deeper levels; or one breaks the outer crust of an exercise that, when first attempted, proved resistant and unyielding.

In working through an exercise, whether alone or in a group, you will sometimes find that writing helps to stimulate the mind when it is sluggish or to center it when it is scattered. But keep in mind that writing is a launching pad to be instantly abandoned once you get off the ground.

Before you start an exercise you must always give yourself some time to seek this disposition: that you embark upon the exercise not for yourself alone but for the welfare of creation, of which you are a part, and that any transformation you experience will redound to the benefit of the world. You will often be surprised to see what a difference it can make when you consciously adopt this attitude.

This book is meant to lead from mind to sense, from thought to fantasy and feeling—then, I hope, through feeling, fantasy, and sense to silence. So use it like a staircase to get up to the terrace. Once there, be sure to leave the stairs, or you will not see the sky.

When you are brought to silence this book will be your enemy. Get rid of it.

Anthony deMello

March 10, 1984.

REALITY

THE CONCLUSION

I imagine that today I am to die.

I ask for time to be alone and write down for my friends
a sort of testament for which the points that follow
could serve as chapter titles.

1. These things I have loved in life:
   Things I tasted,
   looked at,
   smelled,
   heard,
   touched.

2. These experiences I have cherished:

3. These ideas have brought me liberation:

4. These beliefs I have outgrown:

5. These convictions I have lived by:

6. These are the things I have lived for:

7. These insights I have gained in the school of life:
   insights into God,
   the world,
   human nature,

        Jesus Christ,
        love,
        religion,
        prayer.

8. These risks I took,
        these dangers I have courted:

9. These sufferings have seasoned me:

10. These lessons life has taught me:

11. These influences have shaped my life
        (persons, occupations, books, events):

12. These scripture texts have lit my path:

13. These things I regret about my life:

14. These are my life's achievements:

15. These persons are enshrined within my heart:

16. These are my unfulfilled desires:

I choose an ending for this document:
a poem—my own or someone else's;
or a prayer;
a sketch
or a picture from a magazine;
a scripture text;
or anything that I judge would be
an apt conclusion to my testament.

THE VACATION

I imagine I retire to a lonely place
to give myself the gift of solitude,
for solitude is a time when I see things as they are.

What are the little things in life
that lack of solitude has magnified unduly?

What are the really big things
that I find too little time for?

Solitude is the time to make decisions.
What decisions do I need to make
or reconsider
at this juncture of my life?

I now make a decision
about the kind of day today shall be.

Will it be a day of *doing?*
I list the things I really want to do today.

Will it also be a day of *being*
—no effort to achieve,

to get things done,
to gather or possess,
but just to be?
My life will not bear fruit
unless I learn the art of lying fallow,
the art of "wasting" time creatively.

So I decide what time to give to play,
to purposeless and unproductive interests,
to silence, intimacy, rest.
And I ask myself what I shall taste today,
and touch
and smell
and listen to
and see.

THE VENTURE

I imagine I am present
when Jesus first meets Peter
and pronounces him a Rock (John 1:40–42).

I am standing by the lakeside
when he inspires Peter, Andrew, James, and John
to come catch human beings (Matt. 4:18–22).

I walk into the tax house
to hear him summon Matthew
and I witness the effect (Matt. 9:9).

I am present
when the angel tells her destiny to Mary (Luke 1:26–38).

I see the risen Lord send Mary on a mission (John 20:11–18).

When the Voice calls out to Paul
on his journey to Damascus
I am traveling with him (Acts 9:22–26).

> I see these scenes as taking place,
> not in the past,
> but now.
> I do not merely watch,
> I interact . . .
> participate.

I write the story of my own call
for my copy of the Bible.
Like every scripture text,
each word, each phrase is charged with meaning.

I visit Peter in his cell before his execution.
He looks back on the day when Jesus called him,
on the things he saw, and learned,
and felt
—the kind of work, the kind of life he would have had
if Jesus had not met him
—the contrast in today's realities
and yesterday's illusions.

I look back too
on the day when Jesus called me,
just as Peter does.

Then Peter shares his feelings
at the thought that he must die tomorrow.

The call is still alive.
Each day it takes me to I know not what
till after the event.
What was I called to yesterday?

The voice that spoke to Peter at the lakeside
and to Mary at the tomb
—I hear it say to me right now,
"Come . . . I shall send you."

I seem to hear those words
resounding in my heart repeatedly.

I know not what it calls me to,
but I recognize the voice
and I give it my response.

THE ADVENT

The events of history were controlled
for my coming to this world
no less than for the coming of the Savior.
The time had to be ripe,
the place just right,
the circumstances ready,
before I could be born.

God chose the parents of his Son
and endowed them with the personality they needed
for the child that would be born.
I speak to God about the man and woman that he chose
to be my parents
until I see that they had to be
the kind of human beings they were
if I was to become
what God meant me to be.

The Christ child comes, like every other child,
to give the world a message.
What message have I come to give?
I seek guidance from the Lord to express it
in a word
or image.

Christ comes into this world
to walk a certain path,
fulfill a certain destiny.
He consciously fulfilled what had been "written" for him.
As I look back I see in wonder what was "written"
and has thus far been fulfilled
in my own life,
and for each part of that script,
however small,
I say, "Thanks"
to make it holy with my gratitude.

I look with expectation
and surrender
at all that is to come
and, like the Christ,
I say, "Yes. Let it be done."

Finally I recall the song the angels sang
when Christ was born.
They sang of the peace and joy
that give God glory.

Have I ever heard the song the angels sang
when I was born?

I see with joy what has been done through me
to make the world a better place
and I join those angels
in the song they sang
to celebrate my birth.

THE VESSEL

I ask God for a special kind of body
and get the one I have right now.
What thoughts and feelings do I have about this body?

We hear of saints who hated
or were neutral to their bodies.
What attitude is mine?
Where did I get it?

In the blueprint I have drawn up for my life
how does my body help or hinder?

If it could speak,
what would my body say about the blueprint?

My relationship with my body
powerfully affects my life for good or evil.
The finest way to heal,
or deepen, the relationship
is dialogue.

My body must be frank in expressing its resentments—
and its fears—of me.

I must be just as frank.

We keep at it till we are reconciled
and understand and love each other better.

We must then state explicitly
our expectations of each other.

Before we end the dialogue
I ask my body for a word of wisdom.

Scripture reveals my body's spirituality.
It says my body is God's temple,
the spirit's dwelling place.
What does that mean?

It further says our bodies are not ours but Christ's,
so he can say of me, "This is my body."
Again I wonder at the meaning of those words.

I see myself go through the actions of the day
(eating, washing, playing, sleeping)
with the consciousness
that my body is the home of the divine.

Or caring for it
as for the body of my beloved.

Finally I speak to God about my body.
And listen as he speaks to me.

THE WELLSPRINGS

I seek the sources of refreshment,
sustenance, and healing
that my spirit, like my body,
is constantly in need of.

I am made whole again
—my self is given back to me—
in solitude and *silence*.

So now I seek to silence word and thought
by being conscious of the sounds around me,
or the sensations of my body,
or my breathing.

I am energized by *love*.

So I recapture
and relive
the times when I felt loved,
cared for, and treasured.

And I see myself going out in love
to friends,
to those who are in need,
and to every living creature.

I come alive in times of *creativity*.

How does it find expression in my life?

I get peace and *healing*
from my roots in nature.

I recall what happens when I am in harmony
with earth and sky,
with mountains, rivers, oceans,
and nature's many moods
and nature's seasons.

I find everything in *prayer*,
which is for me fragrance and food,
a home, a shield, a tonic.

I recall the seasons of my prayer:
the moments I cry out in despair,
the days of glad thanksgiving,
the times of stillness,
presence,
adoration.

And I recite a prayer or song or poem
that I have come to love,
that I wish to have beside me all through life
and shall want my lips to say when I am dying.

THE LESSON

Jesus says, "The Kingdom is like a mustard seed which a man sowed in his field. Mustard is smaller than any other seed but let it grow and it becomes bigger than any garden plant; it is like a tree, big enough for the birds to come and nest among its branches."

I hold this tiniest of seeds
in the hollow of my hand . . .
then I see the full-grown tree it has become,
strong enough to bear the nests of birds.

I move from seed to tree repeatedly in fantasy.

I then observe the seed
through each stage of its growth.

Finally I sit before the full-grown tree
and speak to it:

We talk about the theme of *smallness,*
the tree and I . . .

About *discouragement* . . .

Risk-taking in our lives . . .

27

Change and all that it implies . . .

Fruitfulness . . .

Service . . .

And finally,
God's power in our lives.

I end this exercise at Jesus's feet:
I tell him what the mustard tree has taught me
and ask that he will teach me too.

THE SECRET

I set out in search
of the source of happiness.

I look minutely at the life
of a happy person who is poor,
then talk with him, attempting to discover
what makes this person happy.

I think of a joyful person in poor health,
in physical pain,
and talk again, searching for what it is
that makes her joyful.

I do the same with a happy person
who has lost his reputation.

I walk into a prison
and am amazed to find a happy person even here.
She tells me what it is
that makes her happy.

Then I observe unhappy people
who are free
and wealthy,
powerful,
respectable.

I talk to them,
and as they talk to me
I listen carefully to their complaints.

Yesterday I had occasions to be happy
that I wasn't even conscious of.
I see them now.

It is inconceivable that anyone
could be grateful and unhappy.
I thank the Lord for each event of yesterday
and notice the effect this has on me.

And the things I call unpleasant, undesirable
—I search for the good that comes from these . . .
the seeds for growth they carry . . .
and find reason to be grateful for them too.

Finally I see myself
moving through each portion of today
in gratitude
—and happiness.

THE CENTER

I imagine that I walk into a desert place.
I spend some time exploring the surroundings,
then settle down to contemplate my life.

I see how frequently I rush outside myself
—to people, occupations, places, things—
in search of strength and peace and meaning,
forgetting that the source of all
is here within my heart.
It is here that I must search.

Each person carries thoughts
that have the power to bring instant peace.
I search for mine.

I also search for the thoughts
that help me face life's challenges
with fortitude and courage.

What are the thoughts that make me warm and gentle,
that exorcise the hate and anger in my heart?

What thoughts put meaning in my life?
produce contentment?
give me joy?
propel me into service?

31

Before I leave the desert
I recall the existence of another source within
that does not need the aid of thoughts
to give me all I need.

I make an indirect attempt to reach it
by imagining a cave within my heart
suffused with light.
The light invades my body as I enter.
I can feel its rays create and energize
and warm and heal.

So I sit within the cave in silent adoration
as the light seeps in through every pore.

THE BIBLE

I become conscious of my breathing
or of sensations in my body,
for this will give me silence
—and God's revealing word
is only understood in silence.

I look at Nature all around me:
the trees, the birds, the animals,
the sky, and the gentle earth.
I think of Nature in her varying moods:
in the freshness of the morning,
the heat of afternoon,
at sunset,
and at dead of night.
I see her specially in her constant movement:
the ever-changing seasons of the year,
the rise and fall of life and death,
her beauty and her violence.

And I ask, "What are you saying to me through Nature, Lord?
What message are you giving me
as I look at her today?"

I wait for God's reply.
It may come in a word, a sentence, or an image,
or a silence that instructs my heart
beyond all words.

If it fails to come
I ask the trees to tell me,
or the birds or stars or rivers
—whatever part of Nature
I happen to be looking at.

I look at human history
—whatever I recall of it
from the Stone Age to our times—
the rise and fall of nations and of cultures,
peace and war,
people good and bad.

And as I look
I wait again for his word to speak to me
in silence.

Through each of the persons I am living with
God breaks into my life.
What is he doing . . .
saying . . .
through them?

I am careful not to rush to put it into words.
I wait till it is "given"
—in language or in silence.

I do the same with life events:
joyful, painful,
sensational, or day-to-day events.

The number is too large.
I could choose to merely see
what happened yesterday
or today,
for from the moment I awoke
—and even while I slept—
God never ceased to act
and to reveal.

So I search, hoping that my eyes will see
and my heart will understand.

> Or I ask the event itself
> to speak to me
> and help me understand.

Before I end I pray
the Lord will give me light
to always understand
the scriptures that he writes today
—my life and every single thing around me.

THE STRANGER

When the Messiah came
his people failed to see him.
He's still around.
When did I see him last?

I think of instances of love I gave
and got.
That was when God became incarnate once again.

Each time that knowledge liberated me
and set me free.
God's word was being revealed again.

The Prophet's burning gaze laid bare our sin
each time my heart flared up
at oppression and injustice,
each time my hidden depths were lit up in a flash
and my defenses were exposed.

At every inner healing I experienced
the Christ reached out and touched me.

And when I felt frustration, darkness, pain,
he struggled in his passion.

The inspiration felt
when I listened to a speech

or read a book
or watched a movie
was the Master calling to discipleship.

And in my prayerful silences
was not the Priest Supreme
uniting God and me?

I search the recent past
to identify these grace-filled moments
and ask that he will come again today.

Then I imagine God anoints me as messiah
and I see myself fulfill this role
in each event that will take place today.

THE ABSOLUTE

God says, "Give me your heart."
And then, in answer to my puzzlement,
I hear him say,
"Your heart is where your treasure is."

My treasures—here they are:
persons . . .
places . . .
occupations . . .
things . . .
experiences of the past . . .
the future's hopes and dreams.

I pick each treasure up,
say something to it,
and place it in the presence of the Lord.

How shall I "give" these treasures to him?

In the measure that my heart is in past treasures
I am fossilized and dead,
for life is only in the present.
So to each of those past treasures,
those golden yesterdays, I say goodbye.
To each I speak, explaining that,

grateful though I am that it came into my life,
it must move out
—or my heart will never learn to love the present.

My heart is in the future too.
Its anxious fears of what will be tomorrow
leave little energy to fully live what is today.
I list these fears
and say to each, "Let the will of God be done,"
observing what effect this has on me,
knowing in my heart
that God can only will my good.

My heart is in my dreams, ideals, hopes,
which make me live in future fiction.
To each of these I say, "Let the will of God be done,
Let him dispose of you as he sees fit."

Having reclaimed the portion of my heart
that was captured by the future and the past,
I now survey my present treasures.

To each beloved person
I say with tenderness, "You are so precious to me,
but you are not my life.
I have a life to live,
a destiny to meet
that is separate from you."

I say to places . . . things . . . I am attached to,
"Precious you are, but not my life.
My life and destiny are separate from you."

I say this to the things
that seem to constitute my very being:
my health,
my ideologies,
my good name, reputation,
and I say it even to my life,
which must succumb some day to death,
"You are desirable and precious,
but you are not my life.
My life and destiny are separate from you."

At last I stand alone before the Lord.
To him I give my heart.
I say, "You, Lord, are my life.
You are my destiny."

THE NOMAD

Jesus says, "A person must be born again
to see God's Kingdom."
To understand this better
I make a study of two worlds.

I contemplate the dark world of the fetus,
then I watch the life of a person who is in love.

I see the pain of human suffering,
then the comfort of the womb.

> I only watch, without reflections,
> for these contrasting scenes alone
> will educate my heart.

I see the world the fetus cannot know:
the glory of the setting sun,
the softness of the night,
the ocean's majesty.

Then my mind runs riot
through scenes of joy
and pain
and fear
and peace
and death
and violence,
contrasting each
with the stillness of the womb.

And a question forms within me:
given the choice, what would I choose—
the ups and downs of life or the comfort of the womb?
My answer will tell
if I have what it takes to be born again.

I can do no more to be born again
than I could to be born the first time.
But two things I can do.

One: I can give myself the nourishment I need.
A child that is born before being formed will perish.
I must stay in touch with the things,
the places,
occupations,
persons
that bring me joy and love and beauty.
I drink deeply at these fountains now
with gratitude,
without guilt.

Two: I can jealously preserve
my freedom and autonomy.

I must learn to hold on
to those fountains that I drink from
and not get stuck;
to enjoy and not possess;
seek nourishment and not sink roots.
For I must always be in readiness
to move when the time for rebirth comes.

And here I squarely face my fear,
for it is fear that kills my freedom
and makes me cling.

I cling to human company
for I fear to be alone;
I cling to popularity
and I fear to give offense;
I cling to friends and family
for I fear to be rejected;
to authority, for I fear being on my own;
to the security of traditional beliefs
and dread to have them challenged.
Finally, I cling to the known,
the familiar, and the old,
for I fear to be reborn
—to move into a world
that is new, unknown, and unfamiliar.

I think how I shall drink of love today,
and joy
and peace
and pleasure.

And I think how I shall seek autonomy and freedom:
the risks I shall dare to take—
the discomforts I shall welcome,
the changes I shall be open to—
as a distant preparation
for the day I shall be born
into another, wider world.

THE OCEAN STAR

I contemplate the wedding feast of Cana
and join in the festivities.
I see how Mary joins in too.
I see her joy,
her thoughtfulness,
and the influence she seems to have on Jesus.

(John 2:1–11)

I go to Lourdes in spirit
and breathe its prayerful atmosphere.

I join the crowds at the miraculous pool,
the grotto of the apparitions,
the blessing of the sick,
the candlelight procession.

I look into the hearts
of the people that I find there:
their dispositions,
expectations,
their attitude to the mother of the Savior.

Then I decide if I, like them,
shall be a devotee and a pilgrim.
What do I do next?

In fantasy I travel
to all the shrines and pilgrim places
where people come to ask for Mary's intercession,
and I think what she has come to mean,
to symbolize
for the disciple of the Lord.

I then go deep within myself
to worship in the temple of my heart.
I stand barefoot and reverent
in the center of this holy place
and decide if I shall build an altar there to Mary.

If I set about constructing it,
I ask myself what function
I shall give her in my life,
what areas I shall place in her protection,
what form of worship I shall offer her.

I search for a word or phrase
to inscribe upon this altar I have built for her.

Or I choose these words
that countless lips have uttered:
"Mother of mercy,
my life,
my sweetness,
and my hope."

RESTORATION

THE REVOLUTION

"Repent and believe the good news," is the theme of Jesus's sermons when he starts his public ministry. I travel with this promising young Prophet as he announces the good news in towns and villages and sense the enthusiasm and hostility he generates by his words and actions.

I am present when he preaches.
I witness the reaction
that his words seem to create
in the hearts of those who hear them
and in my own heart.

When he has finished speaking
someone in the crowd asks what repentance means,
someone else the meaning of the good news.
I listen to his answers.

One day I sit with Jesus all alone
under a tree at noon
or in the house of a friend at night.
He invites me to condense the good news
into three or four sentences.
These sentences must carry news
that puts an end to fear and brings rejoicing
—news so astonishingly good
that one is challenged to believe it.

Then, still seated there with Jesus,
I talk about the word "repent"
—the revolution, the total change of heart and mind.

I imagine Jesus lays his hands on me
to bring about this transformation.

Then I come away
and walk into the day that lies ahead,
transformed in heart and mind,
witnessing the difference this has made
in my behavior
and my feelings.

I see the difference when I pray
or think of death
or read a magazine
or look up at the sky and clouds and trees.

THE DARKNESS

I think of myself as quite a decent person, good-hearted and respected, with minor sins and failings, until it dawns on me that the greatest sinners are the ones who sin in ignorance.

I see the well-intentioned damage
"love" inflicts on helpless children.

I see the marks of cruelty
in fervently religious people.

I see fair-minded Pharisees
assess the evidence against Jesus,
and consider it their duty to do away with him.

It frightens me
that I may be suffering from the sickness
of the chief priests and the Pharisees.

They were so certain of themselves,
so convinced that they were right,
so closed to other viewpoints and to change.
I think of people whom I know to be like that.
And then I think of me.

The Pharisees were given to judging.
People to them were either good or bad.
There was never any good in someone
who their prejudice said was bad.

50

I think of other people who seem to be like that.
I think of me.
I make a list of "bad" people I know
and wonder if at heart they might not be
far better than I am.

The Pharisees were men of the establishment.
They feared to rock the boat.
I think of me.

The Pharisees loved power.
They would force you to be good for your own sake.
They could not leave you free.
Again I think of me.

Finally, the Pharisee conformed.
He might see the accused before him as not being guilty
but he lacked the holy daring
to stand up to his peers and speak his mind.
I think, regretfully, of my fear to give offense,
to disagree,
my need to please.

I am no great improvement
on the men who killed the Savior.
All I can say is, "Lord, I am a sinner.
Be merciful to me."

I hear him answer gently,
"You are precious to my heart, my child."
Whatever could he mean by that?

I use his eyes to find out what he sees in me
that, even while he knows my sinfulness,
he says, "You are precious to my heart."

51

With those same eyes I look at "sinners"
—the Hitlers and the Stalins of our times.

I look at people I dislike . . . reject.

Maybe I need those eyes of his
to bring me to compassion
and save me from the Pharisee in me.

THE ENLIGHTENMENT

When I try to change what I dislike in me
by fighting it
I merely push it underground.
If I accept it,
it will surface and evaporate.
What I resist
will stubbornly persist.

I consider the example of Jesus, who sets himself the task of
moving mountains and battles with exasperating foes. Yet
even in his anger he is loving—he combines a keen desire for
change with an acceptance of reality as it is.

I try to be like him.
I start with feelings I dislike.
To each of them I talk
in a loving, accepting kind of way
and listen to what each has to say,
till I discover that, while it can do me harm,
it also does me good,
that it is there for a benign purpose,
which I now attempt to see.

I keep on with the dialogue
till I feel a real acceptance of these feelings
—acceptance, not approval, not resignation—
so that I am no longer depressed about my depressions

or angry with my anger
or discouraged because of my discouragement
or frightened of my fears
or rejecting of my feelings of rejection.
I can live with them in peace
for I have seen that God can use them for my good.

I do the same
with some of the many other things about my life
that I want to change:

My body's disabilities . . .

My personal shortcomings . . .

The external circumstances of my life . . .

The happenings of the past . . .

The persons with whom I live . . .

The whole world as it is . . .

Old age, sickness, death.

I speak to them with love
and the consciousness that they somehow fit
into God's plan.

In doing so I undergo a transformation:
while everything about me is the same
—the world, my family, my feelings,
my body, my neuroses—

I am the same no longer.
I am more loving now,
more accepting of what is undesirable.
More peaceful, too,
for having come to see
that violence cannot lead to lasting change
—only love and understanding can.

THE REVELATION

I imagine myself to be in the presence of Christ
and expose myself to it in silence,
for it heals . . .
creates . . .
encourages.

I now ask him to give me
as complete a list as possible
of everything in me he finds defective—
each indication of my selfishness,
each area I have yet to grow in,
each thing in me I need to change.

> And as he speaks
> I make a mental note of what he says
> —I even write it down
> if I judge that this will help.

Then I ask him which of these defects,
in his opinion,
needs the most urgent attention.

> I let myself go blank for a few seconds
> and imagine that he speaks,
> and I am careful to be open to the fact
> that what he says may be totally unexpected.

I turn my gaze within
to see if I have the will
to change this defect.
If I do not, then I take this lack of will
as the first thing to be changed.

Now I begin with the most essential element
to all change.
Before I take a single step,
it is vital that I hear Christ say these words to me:
"As far as my love for you is concerned
it does not matter whether you change or not,
for my love for you is unconditional."

Now I see Christ's power flooding into me
and I imagine I feel strong where before I was afraid,
relaxed where formerly I was tense,
outgoing in places where I used to be withdrawn.

I see myself going through the day
(or into a situation where this new power is needed)
equipped with this power received from Christ.

Finally I rest in his loving presence
in grateful adoration.

THE SATELLITE

I look at nature and reflect on the existence in it of a force so silent and invisible that human beings were not aware of it till lately; and yet so mighty that the world is moved by it: the force of gravity.

Because of it the bird flies in the sky,
mountains are held in place,
leaves flutter to the ground,
planets are kept in orbit.

There is no better symbol of God's power
and presence.

Scenes of suffering flash through my mind:
torture chambers;
concentration camps;
the ravages of famine;
scenes of war,
of hospitals,
and of accidents.
And I see him there as silent and invisible as gravity.

I conjure up a thousand painful scenes
from the history of my life:
of boredom and frustration;
of pain, anxiety, rejection;

of meaninglessness and despair;
and in every scene I sense his silent presence.

I see his power like gravity
in every nook and corner of the world:
no place in space,
no point in time
escapes, for it is all-pervasive.

Then I see his love to be like gravity:
I hear Paul's cry that nothing in creation
can wrench us from God's love (Rom. 8:31–39).

I remember with emotion
the times I fought his love
—in vain, for love is irresistible!

I see that God has never ceased to draw my heart.
The pull, like gravity, could not be felt.
But at some blessed moments
that I now recall with joy
the tug could not be missed.

When was the pull last felt?

Not yesterday? Why not?

I end by letting go,
succumbing to this power of divinity,
as my body does to gravity.

THE FIND

Jesus says, "Here is a picture of the Kingdom. It is like a treasure buried in a field. The man who found it went and, through sheer joy, sold everything he had—and bought that field."

I have a treasure:
the thing I value most in life.
I relive the events
that led me to discover it.

I think of the history of my life
from the time I found this treasure . . .
what it has done for me
and meant to me.

I stand before this treasure
(God or Jesus Christ
or a conviction, value, or ideal
or a person, task, or mission)
and I say, "Of all the things I have,
you are the dearest."
And I see what happens to me
when I pronounce that sentence.

I think how much I would gladly do
or give (even life itself, maybe)
in order to preserve this treasure.

If it is not that important, I acknowledge this with sadness
—and I hope for a day when I shall find a treasure for
which through sheer joy I shall be ready to give up
everything.

I am a treasure.
Someday, somewhere, someone discovered me.
I should have no awareness of my worth
if someone had not found it.
I recall and relive the details of the finding.

I am a multifaceted treasure.
There were many things concealed in me
that different people drew out
and revealed to me.
I joyfully review each one of these
and gratefully remember the persons who uncovered them.

Finally I stand before the Lord
and find, to my surprise,
that he considers me a treasure.
I see reflected in his eyes the many lovely facets
that only he could have observed in me
and I rest in the love he gives me.

THE HEART

I imagine that I walk into a church at night
for adoration of the blessed sacrament.
The candles on the altar
are the only source of light.
I rest my eyes upon the host
that stands out clear and white
against the darkness.

The host is like a magnet,
for it draws my eyes and being
toward itself as to the center.
Most of my life I focus on the outer surface,
but here I gaze into the very heart of things,
the center of my being and of the world.

As I keep looking at the host
a silence falls upon me.
All thinking quiets down and fades away.
The silence of that host seems to seep into my body
and from there it spreads throughout the church,
so everything inside me
and around
is stilled.

Then as I look
the host begins to send out rays of light

that enter me
and I am grateful, for I know
that they will flood my mind
and my unconscious,
cleansing me from all that is self-centered
and perverse and grasping and afraid.

And while the darkness of the church is undisturbed
the darkness in my heart is put to flight
and all of me is made transparent.

The rays now bring with them a holy energy
that soaks into my body
and fortifies my spirit
to face up to the challenges of life.

And with this energy a fire spreads all over me
to purify my heart
of hatred, bitterness, resentment
and give me power to love.

So I avidly expose my heart
to this life-producing sun
that shines out at the center
of the dark and silent church.

THE DESERT

I look at Jesus in his agony
on the night before he died.

I stand quite close to him
and watch him reaching out for human help,
but no one now can reach him
—he is entirely on his own before he dies.

I contrast this
with the warmth and closeness
of the supper room
where he had been a little while before.

As I watch I realize
that people will ultimately come to terms
with God, with destiny, and with themselves
only when they dare to seek aloneness.

I give myself a taste
of what it means to be alone.

I am living in a desert:
no books . . . no occupation . . .
no sound of human voice
—for a whole day . . . a week . . . for months.
I see how I react
when I am thrown back on my own resources,
when I am stripped of what I mostly use

to run away from looking at myself:
work and human company.

Then I see myself in a solitary prison cell:
soundproof walls, a narrow room,
the dim light of a bulb all day . . .
never the glimpse of a human face
or of any living thing,
or sun or sky . . .
never a sound of human voice or nature
for weeks . . . for months on end . . .
not knowing when it will end.

Finally—I have lapsed into a coma:
I can hear the words of people
and feel their touch
but cannot reach them.

Now I return to life:
to my worries and my work,
my comforts and attachments,
the world of human beings,
but I realize that I am not the same
from having been exposed
to the rigors of aloneness.

Every now and then my heart returns
to Jesus in his agony.
I watch him as he grapples with his God
and with his destiny,
and the sight gives me a wisdom
that thinking never could.
So I linger there and look.

THE VOLCANO

I look to gurus, writers, friends, surroundings
to give me peace or fortitude or meaning in my life.
But these external agents can never be a substitute
for inner, deeper sources.

I search for these interior sources.
I imagine that I make a journey
to the deepest level of my being.
Everything inside is dark.
No trace of that interior light
the mystics speak of!
When I reach the very center
I see an upward spurting flame,
the symbol of a holy fire
of which I am generally quite unconscious.

There is a rhythm
to the spurting of that flame,
and I hear a word or mantra
being chanted to that rhythm
—a word like the name of Jesus
or a mantra like "My God and my all,"
or "Abba, Father,"
or "Come, Holy Spirit,"
or whatever.
I listen till I seem to hear the chant.

If I have heard the mantra
on some former inward journey,
I might imagine
that I hear it once again,
or I might hear
some other word or sentence
at this time.

Once I have heard the mantra
I chant it in my heart.
With every recitation
a deep, mysterious peace
comes from the center of my being
and spreads till it invades the whole of me.

The peace spreads through my stomach
and my head and neck
and arms and legs
and every member of my body.
Now every time I say the holy word
the peace within me deepens.
It is as if with every recitation I let go,
I relax my being into the hands of God.

Now a quiet strength takes hold of me
each time I say the mantra,
an energy that spreads all over me
together with a sense of confidence,
of I-can-do-all-things-in-him-who-strengthens-me.

And all anxieties begin to fade.
I see myself in situations
that I formerly avoided
from timidity and fear
—the mantra makes me confident and strong.

To end the exercise I go down once again
to the center of my being
to seek the warmth that comes
from that interior fire
and to rest in the holy strength my mantra gives.

THE ASSENT

I recall the words of Jesus as he left the supper room,
"So that the world may know I love the Father, let us go."
To love the Father—that, for Jesus,
meant surrender to his will at every moment.

I look at this surrender in his passion.
He seems to have had a premonition
of the kind of death that would be his.
I see him sitting all alone
some days before his death,
reviewing every detail of his suffering,
and to each of those events, foreseen by him,
I hear him say, "Let it be done."

I contemplate the passion of humanity:
the countless faces ravaged by depression,
loneliness,
and fear.

And bodies racked with pain:
the accidents
and hospitals
and concentration camps
and torture chambers.
And at each scene
I hear Christ saying to his Father,
"Let it be done."

Each time I find myself revolting
at this spectacle of suffering,
I recall the revolt of Jesus in his agony
and, even while I do all in my power
to take away the suffering,
I learn, like him, to say,
"Let it be done."

Finally I look at my own life:
at everything in it that is meaningless
and wasteful
and frustrating.

At all the suffering I have had
whether caused by me
or others
or by life itself.

And as each scene appears before my mind, I say,
"Let it be done."

I look into the vast, uncertain future:
into my passion
and my death.
And to everything that lies in store for me
I say, "Let it be done."

THE COMMISSION

I recall the scene of Jesus sending his disciples out
to preach the Kingdom,
to heal
and cast out demons (Luke 10:1–12).

I am there when he announces
the names of those who will be sent.
What do I feel when I hear him call my name?
and when I think of moving out to unfamiliar places?

What preparations do I make
to go out on my mission?

Prior to setting out
each one is given a private meeting
with the Lord.
When I see his loving look I sense, to my dismay,
that I am moving out to change the world
with a heart that sadly needs a change itself!

How shall I bring peace to others
when there is conflict in my heart?
The conflict between what I really am
and what I seem to be,
between what I practice and what I preach,
and the deepest conflict of them all:
between what I want to do, and be,

71

and have happen in my life
—and what God wants.

Shall I set captives free
when my heart is in the grip
of inordinate attachments,
anxieties for the future,
and guilt about the past?

I am going to teach forgiveness
when I am bitter and resentful.

To give to others a passion for the truth
—while I am so defensive—
and hold on stubbornly to my views,
refusing to be open.

What courage shall I offer others
when I am such a coward—even in trifles,
for I fear so much to hurt,
to turn down a request,
to disagree . . .
and dread unpleasantness and opposition.

I am setting out to teach compassion
—and I am ever eager to condemn.
I lack the Lord's own gentleness of heart,
for I see deliberate malice
where he sees ignorance and weakness.

I came enthusiastically
to get the blessing of the Lord before starting on my mission.
Now I am discouraged:

how shall I create a revolution,
never having experienced one myself?

I say to him, "Don't send me.
I am not worthy."

What does he say to that?

THE HAZARD

I recall the words of Paul,
"Let this mind be in you
which was in Jesus Christ."

I ask the Lord to offer me his heart.
I see him take away my heart of stone,
put in its place his heart of flesh.

I feel the strange sensation
of returning to my world
with someone else's heart.

I sense in me an urge to pray.
I hurry to my usual place of prayer
and feel my new heart doing unusual things.

I walk along a busy street.
The usual crowds are everywhere
and I look at them, to my astonishment,
in a strangely different kind of way today.
The sight of them awakens thoughts and feelings
quite different from the ones I am accustomed to.

I set out for my home
and as I walk I look at trees and birds,
at clouds and animals and all of nature
with a different kind of vision.

At home,
at work,
I look at people I dislike
and see myself reacting differently.
The same thing happens
with the people to whom I formerly felt neutral.
And I realize, to my surprise, that I am different
even with the ones I love.

I notice that with this new heart of mine
I am strong in situations
that I formerly avoided.

There are occasions
when my heart dissolves in tenderness
and others when it burns with indignation.

My new heart makes me independent:
I do not cease to be attached to many things,
but the clinging disappears
—I feel free to let them go.
I try this out delightedly,
moving from one attachment to another.

Then, to my alarm, it steers me into situations
that get me into trouble.
I find myself involved in things
that put an end to my desire for comfort.
I say things that antagonize.

Finally I come back to the presence of the Lord
to give him back his heart.
It was exciting to be fitted
with the heart of Christ himself.

But I know I am not ready for it yet.
I still need to protect myself a little.

But even as I take my poor heart back
I know that I will be a different person
from having felt, if only for a moment,
what it meant to have this heart, this mind in me
that was in Jesus Christ our Lord.

THE EVIDENCE

I am in a very dark room
and Jesus Christ appears to me.
The apparition grows brighter by degrees
till it casts a glow all over,
transforming every object
into a thing of beauty.

As I expose myself to that transforming presence
I see myself transfigured.
And for a while I contemplate the parts of me
that have been made resplendent.

The presence indicates a wall
on which I see a vision:
I am shown the good that I have done
and has been done through me
at every stage of my existence.

The vision changes
and areas I have grown in
are now revealed to me:
fears dispelled,
ill feelings overcome,
"impossibilities" made possible.

On that illumined screen
I see the loveliness of all my life at every stage:
infancy . . . childhood . . . adolescence.

And I am made to understand in symbols
what my existence means.
Images keep flashing on that screen
while I look on in joy and wonder.
I count at least a dozen.

And last of all
I am shown the beauty and the meaning
of the day that lies ahead of me.

The screen now disappears
and I am conscious of the presence of the Lord
till that too fades away
and I am all alone in darkness,
with a heart that has been brought to life
by what has been revealed to it.

THE KING

Moments after Jesus has died I stand on the hill of Calvary,
unconscious of the crowd. It is as if I am alone, my eyes fixed
on that lifeless body on the cross.

I watch the thoughts and feelings
that arise within me
as I look.

I see the crucified as stripped of everything:

Stripped of his dignity,
naked before his friends and enemies.

Stripped of his reputation.
My mind goes back to scenes and times
when he was spoken well of.

Stripped of success.
I recall the heady years
when his miracles were acclaimed
and it seemed as if the Kingdom
were about to be established.

Stripped of credibility.
So he could not come down from the cross.
So he could not save himself
—he must have been a fraud.

Stripped of support.
Even the friends who did not run away
are powerless to reach him.

Stripped of his God
—the God he thought of as his Father,
who he hoped would save him in his hour of need.

Finally I see him stripped of life,
this existence here on earth
that he, like us, held on to tenaciously
and was unwilling to let go of.

As I gaze at that lifeless body I slowly understand
that I am looking at the symbol
of supreme and total liberation.
In being fastened to the cross
Jesus becomes alive and free.
Here is a parable of conquest, not defeat.
It calls for envy, not commiseration.

So now I contemplate the majesty of the man
who has freed himself
from all that makes us slaves,
destroys our happiness.

In gazing at that freedom
I think with sadness of my slavery.

I am a slave to public opinion.
I think of the times I am controlled
by what society will say and think of me.

I am driven to success.
I see the times I run away from challenges and risks
—because I hate to make mistakes or fail.

I am enslaved by the need for human consolation:
How many times I was dependent
on the approval and acceptance of my friends
and their power to assuage my loneliness . . .
the times I was possessive of my friends
and lost my freedom.

I think of my enslavement to my God.
I think of the times I try to use him
to make my life secure
and undisturbed and painless.
Also the times I am enslaved by fear of him
and by the need to protect myself against him
through rites and superstitions.

Finally I think of how I cling to life,
how paralyzed I am by fears of every kind,
unable to take risks
for fear of losing friends or reputation,
success or life or God.

And so I gaze in admiration at the crucified
who won his final liberation in his passion
when he fought with his attachments,
let go of them,
and conquered.

I see the lines of people everywhere
who will kneel today, Good Friday,
in adoration of the crucified.
I perform my adoration here on Calvary,
completely unaware of the noisy crowd around me:
I kneel and touch my forehead to the ground,
desiring for myself

the freedom and the victory
that shine out in that body on the cross.

And in my adoration
I hear those haunting words re-echo in my heart:
"If you wish to follow me,
you must follow with your cross."
And those other words, "Unless it dies,
the grain of wheat remains alone."

CHRIST

THE ENCOUNTER

My relationship with Jesus Christ
is of paramount importance,
for I am his disciple.
In this exercise I seek to deepen the relationship.

I imagine I am told that I will meet him
on a solitary mountaintop
and I set out for the place at once.
What feelings rise within me when I think
that I shall soon be meeting Jesus Christ?

In my mountain solitude I am gazing at the plains below.
Then I become aware that he is here.
In what way does he show himself to me?
And what are my reactions to his presence?

I talk to him about our friendship.

It is best to start with what is negative.
The negative feelings one ordinarily has
toward friends are mainly two:
resentment and fear.

I resent my friends when they become a burden
—when they make demands on me

that I do not want to meet;
when they become possessive;
curb my freedom;
deny me what I want or need.

If resentments lurk within me,
my relationship stands to gain
by my becoming conscious of them.
So I ask myself if Jesus is a burden:
is he the kind of friend whose complaints
produce guilt feelings,
who puts pressure on me,
makes demands I am not ready for,
curtails my freedom by possessiveness?
If so, I tell him this quite openly
and hear him answer,
till I see that it is not he
but my distorted image of him
that has done the mischief.

Fear is the other negative emotion:
I let Jesus explain that if I fear him
I have yet to understand love's unconditionality,
that to feel loved unconditionally is to know
that perfect love puts an end to fear.

Having resolved our differences,
we move on to examining the relationship in itself.

What adjectives would best describe our friendship?
They may be negative, ambiguous, even contradictory,
but if they fit

they will help to deepen the relationship
by the insights they will offer.

Or what analogies?
He and I decide
what images are best designed
to symbolize our friendship.

From the present we move to the past.
I think what Jesus Christ was to me in my childhood
and at various stages of my growth.
I think of the ups and downs
that our relationship has known.

Our relationship calls for one more thing:
I explicate my expectations of him
—what I expect him to do for me
and be to me
and what I want from him.

And I ask what he expects of me.

The time has come for him to go,
so he and I look at the future.
What kind of future do we want
our relationship to have?
Is there something concrete I can do about this?

The presence fades away
and I linger on the mountain
to savor for a while the mood
that meeting Jesus has induced in me.

THE OFFER

I call to mind the times
when Jesus Christ said, "Come!"
to people in the gospel.
I imagine that I hear that word
addressed to me today
and I respond to it.

When two of John's disciples
asked Jesus where he lived,
he said, "Come and see."
I talk with him about the things that I have seen
since the day he first invited me
to be with him,
the things that he has shown me.

I then recall the words of Philip,
"Show us the Father
—that is all we want."
Is there anything I still desire him to show me?

To each of his disciples Jesus said,
"Come, follow me."
I ask myself what following him has done for me
over the years.

Another "Come":
Jesus says to fishermen by the lake,
"Come and I shall get you to catch human beings."
I think of the inspiration
I have sometimes brought to others.
I think of those whose goodness or whose talents
I have drawn out by my love.
I think of the times when I brought faith
where there was fear,
solace where there was pain,
love to replace indifference,
peace to temper violence.
I think of those who were absorbed in daily trifles
until, because of me,
they heard a call to something greater.
And I rest in the sound of his words,
"Come, and I shall get you to catch human beings."

"Come to me all you who are tired and weary
and I shall give you rest."
An invitation to find my rest in him!
What words spring to my lips
when I hear him say those words to me?

And finally, "Anyone who is thirsty
should come to me and drink."
How does one slake one's thirst
on Jesus Christ?

THE LORD

I think of the impact Jesus Christ has had
on human history . . .

And on my life.

Then I conduct a dialogue with him.

I tell him what it is about him
that appeals to me the most
and listen to what he says in reply.

I tell him which of his words
have had the greatest impact on me
and how those words have influenced my life.

His disciples sometimes speak
of his presence in their lives.
I ponder on the meaning that word "presence" has for me.
In what way, if at all, has he been present in my past
and in my life today?

He indicated he was sent to teach us how to love.
What kind of love has Jesus taught me?
If I am a loving person,
to what extent is he responsible?

He also claimed he was sent to bring liberation
to the lives of people.

Has this been my experience?
Or have I, on the contrary, felt constricted
and oppressed
by his demands
and teachings?
Or have I experienced both
oppression and liberation simultaneously?
In what specific areas?

Before I end my dialogue I ask myself
what impact Jesus had on yesterday.

And I tell him what I think
his influence will be
on what I think and say and do today.

THE CREATOR

I seek a place in fantasy
where I can be alone with Jesus Christ.
What feelings and reactions does this create in me?

The topic of my talk with him today is faith.

Faith is the assent of the mind
to a truth revealed by God.
From among the many truths about Jesus Christ
presented in the scriptures
I choose a few
that I have found to be meaningful to me.

Then I talk to him
about this special creed I have composed.

Faith concerns the word, the promise of another.
How many of the promises of Jesus
do I have faith in?
I talk to him about this too.

To have faith means to trust.
Do I trust Jesus Christ?
I tell him what this means to me in practice.

If I am Jesus's disciple it is not enough
that I have faith in him.
It is equally important that he have faith in me.

A friend calls forth, creates,
a quality that he sees in me
—it is thus that a lover creates his beloved,
a Master his disciple.

Does Jesus have this kind of faith in me?
What has he seen and brought to light in me?
I imagine that I hear him tell me.

When Jesus first set eyes
on Peter, the Fearful, the Impulsive,
he saw in him what no one
would have thought was there
and nicknamed him the Rock
—so Peter changed eventually,
becoming what the nickname said he was.
What kind of name or names does Jesus find for me?
I listen
and react to what he says.

THE RECOGNITION

In my prayer today I face a vital question:
who is Jesus Christ for me?

I begin by imagining myself to be in his presence
—a presence that allows me to be totally myself.
I then conduct a dialogue with him,
taking for subject matter
the titles scripture gives him.

The first one is connected with his name: *Savior.*
Has Jesus been a savior to me?
In what circumstances?
On what occasions?
When I address him by this title,
what meaning does it have?

I share with him my answers to these questions.
He responds.

Another title scripture bestows on him is *Lord.*
I tell him what it means to me to call him Lord
and he comments.

The scriptures call him *Teacher.*
I ponder on the lessons he has taught me
and ask him how he sees my role as pupil.

Here are titles Jesus gave himself:
I am the *Resurrection*
and the *Life.*
Can Jesus claim to be my life?
What meaning does that have
in my everyday existence?

He also gave himself the title *Friend:*
"You are my friends
because I have revealed everything I know to you."
What are these revelations
he has made to me in friendship?

I put aside the scriptures now
and let my heart express its own experience of him
in a title of its own creation.
And I observe how he responds to it.

THE RESPONSE

I listen to the sounds around me,
the better to prepare myself
to listen to the gospel.

I now hear Jesus say to me
some of the sentences he said
to people in the gospels.
He says, "Who do you say that I am?"

> I do not reply to those words at first.
> I let them echo and re-echo in my ears
> for quite some time,
> observing how my heart reacts to them.

> And only when I can restrain myself no longer
> do I react to them
> —in just one word
> or silence.

I do the same with other gospel phrases:

"Do you love me?"

"Come, follow me."

"So long a time have I been with you
and you do not know me?"

"Do you believe?
Everything is possible to one who believes."

THE PIONEER

I begin with a careful reading of Luke 4:14–30:
the return of Jesus to his hometown.

I look at the village of Nazareth:
its location, the homes,
the synagogue, the village well.

I see the excitement as word goes round
that the young prophet is coming home.
I see the skepticism, too.
Jesus creates division even in his hometown,
even in his absence.

He divides not just the good people from the bad,
but good people among themselves,
for I observe people who are against him in good faith,
people who seem to have good reason to oppose him.
I listen to the arguments of one such person
who doesn't seem a bad sort at all.

I am seated in the crowded synagogue
and sense the tension, the expectancy,
as Jesus reads a passage from the scroll
and comments on it.
Even those who are against him

seem taken up by the words of grace
that flow from him.
I am delighted that he has won them over.

And I am distressed when he goes on to offend them.
Why is he bent on confrontation?

I see the fury of the crowd
and I look on sadly
as he is pushed out of the village.

I am sitting all alone with Jesus now,
after the event.
I, the disciple, am full of questions.
He, the Master, answers.
"Where do you get your courage from?" I ask,
and, "Do you ever feel afraid?"

Then, "Why do you antagonize them?"

"How is it that your own people
fail to recognize you?"

"Am I one of those who fail to recognize?"
In reply he shows me people I am living with
whose holiness I fail to see
because I focus overmuch
on their shortcomings and defects.
He also points to some events at random,
opening my eyes to see
that they are charged with grace,
which I failed to recognize
because they seemed so commonplace.

My final question:
"Will I ever get in touch, Lord,
with the source from which your words
and wisdom flow?
Will I ever find
the wellsprings of your courage?"
What does he say to that?

THE PROMISE

It was the custom in the past
for saints to practice
what they called spiritual communion
—communion through desire.

I attempt to do the same.
I imagine the scene of the Last Supper
as if I am present there myself.

I observe Jesus as he takes bread in his hands,
blesses and distributes it.
When I receive it from his hands
I think what I want this bread to be for me.

Then Jesus speaks with us, his disciples.
His words are an essential part
of the eating of that bread,
so I listen carefully.

He first gives us a new command
—to love one another as he has loved us.
I pray that this bread will increase
my capacity to love
and I think what love has come to mean for me
and what place I give it in my life.

If we eat this bread,
this body that is broken,
we shall necessarily share
in the passion and death of Jesus.
I hear him prophecy that we will be persecuted,
even by our own.
So I pray for the courage that sustained the martyrs
and the strength to live and speak as he did.

He makes a gift at this holy meal: peace.
Not the peace of the world, he says,
but his peace.
I ponder on the meaning of those words
and I ask for that gift for me
and for those I love.

Then he makes us a promise.
We will be in pain, he says,
and the world will rejoice,
"but I shall come back to you
and your hearts will be filled with joy
and no one will be able
to take that joy from you."
I pray that through this bread that I have eaten
I shall forever experience
the joy-giving presence of the risen Lord
in all the ups and downs of life.
I imagine scenes of the future
where I shall need this presence
and I trust he will be there.

He then begins to pray for us.
I listen and I make his prayer my own.
He prays that we will all be one
as he and his Father are one,
that this will be the sign
by which the world will know

that he has come from God.
I pray that this bread will be a force for unity
in every group where it is eaten.

Jesus speaks long and late into the night.
Supper is finally over.
Now he takes a cup of wine.
I listen to the words he utters over it.
The cup is passed from hand to hand
and when it is my turn to drink
I pray that I shall be intoxicated
and lose myself in love.

LIFE

THE REDEMPTION

I become aware of my presence in this room,
of the sensations I experience in my body,
of the touch of the clothes I am wearing,
and the chair I am sitting on.
I become aware of the sounds all around me
and of my breathing.

And I advert to the fact that I am living.

I imagine a fully alive plant or animal . . .
I think of a person who is fully alive.
What qualities do I find in this person?
For me, what does it mean to be fully alive?

One thing is certain:
to be fully alive involves the renunciation
of one's past and of one's future.

The past. Yesterday.
I cannot be alive if I cling to yesterday
for yesterday is a memory,
a creation of the mind.
It is not real.
So to live in yesterday is to be dead.

I therefore let go of my yesterdays,
my propensity for living in the past.

One way of living in the past
is holding on to grievances.
As a first step toward being fully in the present
I make a list of people I resent.
I offer each of them an amnesty, an absolution,
and let them go.

The absolution will not come
if I feel that they alone are guilty,
I am blameless.
I must see myself as being coresponsible
with the offender
for each offense that I have been the victim of.

It is difficult to absolve a person whose offense
I see as being a total evil.
The fact is his offense has done me good.
He was an instrument used by God to bring me grace,
as Judas was an instrument used by God
to bring grace to humanity and Jesus Christ.

If I mean to give up living in the past
I must drop regrets
as cleanly as I drop resentments.
What I tend to look upon as loss—
my failings,
my mistakes,
my handicaps,
the lack of opportunities in my life,
my so-called bad experiences—
I must learn to see them all as blessings.
For in the dance of life
all things cooperate to do us good.

Having let go of resentments and regrets
I also let go of my good experiences.
Experiences, like worldly goods, can be accumulated,

and if I cling to them
I shall once again be living in the past.
So I say goodbye to persons . . .
places . . .
occupations . . .
things . . . that I treasure from the past.
We shall never meet again
because when I return they will have changed,
I will have changed,
all will be different.
So, goodbye . . .
thank you and goodbye.

I have let go of my yesterdays.
I have still to dispossess myself of my tomorrows,
for the future, like the past, is dead
—a construction of the mind—
and to live in it is to be dead to here and now.
So I renounce my greed and all ambition
to acquire,
to achieve,
to become somebody in the future.
Life is not tomorrow; life is now.
So is love
and God
and happiness.

I think of things
I am greedy and ambitious for (tomorrow)
and imagine that I push them all away.
A blessed relief, for when I drop my greed
I drop my bondage to anxiety
and am freed to be alive.
I take a while to let myself experience this relief
and freedom.

Having released myself
from the future and the past,
I come into the present
to experience life as it is now,
for eternal life is now,
eternal life is here:
I listen to the sounds around me . . .
I become aware of my breathing in and out
and of my body
so as to be as fully present as I can.

THE EXPOSURE

I think of the times I come alive
and the times when I am dead.

I ponder on the features I assume
in moments of aliveness
and in times when I am dead.

Life abhors security:
for life means taking risks,
exposing self to danger,
even death.
Jesus says that those who wish to be safe will lose their lives;
those who are prepared to lose their lives will keep them.

I think of the times
when I drew back from taking risks,
when I was comfortable and safe:
those were times when I stagnated.

I think of other times
when I dared to take a chance,
to make mistakes,
to be a failure
and a fool,
to be criticized by others,
when I dared to risk being hurt

110

and to cause pain to others.
I was alive!

Life is for the gambler.
The coward dies.

Life is at variance with my perception
of what is good and bad:
these things are good and to be sought;
these others bad and to be shunned.
To eat of the Tree of Knowing Good and Bad
is to fall from paradise.
I must learn to accept whatever life may bring,
pleasure and pain, sorrow and joy.
For if I close myself to pain
my capacity for pleasure dies
—I harden myself
and repress what I regard as unpleasant and undesirable,
and in that hardness, that repression,
is rigidity and death.

So I decide to taste in all its fullness
the experience of the present moment,
calling no experience good or bad.
Those experiences that I dread—I think of them,
and, inasmuch as I am able, I let them come
and stop resisting them.

Life goes hand in hand with change.
What does not change is dead.
I think of people who are fossils.
I think of times when I was fossilized:
no change, no newness,
the same old worn-out concepts
and patterns of behavior,

the same mentality, neuroses,
habits, prejudices.

Dead people have a built-in fear of change.
What changes have there been in me
over the past six months?
What changes will there be today?

I end this exercise
by watching nature all around me:
so flexible,
so flowing,
so fragile,
insecure,
exposed to death
—and so alive!

I watch for many minutes.

THE KINGDOM

I imagine that I enter a deep dark cave
where I am totally alone.
I sit down in a corner
to meditate on life.

Today I choose to see life in its brokenness
and uselessness
and waste.

I imagine flowers growing by a roadside
and I see the seeds
that never made it to the surface of the ground,
the tender shoots
that sprouted only to be trampled on by people,
devoured by cattle, scorched by the heat of the sun.
At every stage of growth
thousands must perish
for one flower that will bloom.

I see trillions of wasted eggs
and fetuses destroyed
and babies born to perish
for every human that survives.

113

I see the wasted struggles of millions
who aspire to be actors,
writers,
political leaders,
saints,
and end in failure . . .
for the handful that arrives.

I have myself arrived at where I am today
through countless wasted hours of boredom,
useless conversations,
pastimes,
incapacitating sickness,
or sufferings I was fool enough to bring upon myself.
Through energy I squandered
on unproductive planning,
stillborn projects,
fruitless undertakings.

I contemplate the myriad opportunities I threw away,
the talents I neglected,
the challenges I dared not face,
the promises that never were
and, worse still, never will be kept.

> I contemplate this not with sadness,
> not with guilt,
> but with patient understanding,
> for I wish to love life as much in its failure
> as in its success.

And I recall the parable the Lord gave us
as a symbol of the Kingdom:

The sower goes out to sow his seed;
some of it falls on rocky soil,
some among thorns and thistles,
some on the road where it is trampled on
or eaten by the birds,
and some of it bears a hundredfold
or maybe less, just thirtyfold or sixty.

And I love the whole of that field.
I love the rock
and the fertile soil,
the pathway
and the thorns and thistles,
for all of it is part of life.
I love the seed that is sensationally fruitful
and the seed that has just average success.
Today I especially love
the seed that is sown only to perish
so that before it goes into oblivion
it will be blessed and redeemed by my love.

Finally I look at the Savior on the cross,
symbolizing in his broken body
and his unsuccessful mission
the drama of life in general
and my life in particular.
I love him too,
and as I press him to my heart
I understand that somewhere, somehow,
all of it has a meaning,
all of it is redeemed
and made beautiful
and resurrected.

THE MENDICANT

When I think how long I have lived
I am struck by life's injustice:
others have lived much less
(I think of some I have known),
some have been given less than an hour of life.

I recall my childhood
and the various stages of my growth.
I have been blessed, indeed, beyond anything
I expected or deserved!

I think of the experiences that life has given me
—happy ones that filled my heart,
painful ones that helped me grow—

Of the discoveries I have made . . .

Of the persons I was privileged to meet . . .

And of my talents and abilities,
of sight
and hearing,
smell and taste and touch
and mind and will and memory
and the limbs and organs of my body.

If I were to die today
I should certainly have had more than my fair share

of life's blessings.
Whatever else life has in store for me is an added gift
—quite undeserved.

Having accepted this, I make myself aware of the fact
that I have another day of life to live and relish.
I see myself go through the morning,
the afternoon,
and evening,
and accept my good luck gratefully.

I think of the person who to me is the dearest
of all who are alive today,
of how he or she has enriched my life.

Tomorrow I may lose her . . .
such is life's fragility.

And if I did, I should have no cause for complaint.
I have had her for so long,
God knows I had no right to her for a single hour.
Life has been unjust:
I think of those who never had
the riches she has brought me.
I tell her this in fantasy
and see what happens.

I now become aware
that she is here for yet another day
and I am grateful.

THE DISCOVERY

I imagine I am told that six months hence
I will be blind.
I observe how I react to this.

I make a list of persons . . . places . . . things . . .
that I want to see again,
to stamp them on my memory before I lose my sight.
What feelings do I have
when I attempt to see them now in fantasy?

I now go through an average day—
rising,
traveling,
eating,
reading—
as a blind person,
observing all my thoughts and feelings.

What does blindness do to my profession,
to my relationship with others?

I determine that my life is going to be
as fruitful and as happy
as it was before I lost my sight
and see what this decision does for me.

118

Blind people often come to see things
that they missed when they had sight.
I search for these.

To end this exercise I ponder on the wealth
that sight has brought me.

Would I have been the person that I am today
if I had never seen the sunrise
or the moon
or flowers in bloom
or people's faces?
I let my heart return
to scenes of beauty it has feasted on
thanks to my eyes.

If wonder is the heart of contemplation,
how many mystic moments my eyes have given me!
I seek them out.

I return to scenes of love
and tenderness
I would not have got
—or given—
if it were not for my eyes.

I picture what my life would be
without the knowledge
and the entertainment
reading gave me.

To end, I ask myself
how I shall use my eyes today.

THE AWAKENING

I make believe that I am paralyzed from the shoulders down.
I vividly imagine my surroundings
and notice what my thoughts and feelings are.

I see the changes paralysis has brought about in
my work and my profession,
my relationships,
my self-image,
my attitude to self,
my life of prayer, my relationship with God,
my views on life.
I observe myself reacting, for example, to the daily news,
my attitudes and values regarding work,
time,
achievement,
love,
growth,
life,
progress,
death.

I contemplate an average day
from the moment of my waking in the morning
till I fall asleep at night:
my first thought on awaking,
my meals,

my toilet needs,
my work
and therapy,
my entertainment,
prayer.

At night I dedicate some minutes to thanksgiving.

I am thankful for the gift of speech:
I can express my needs
and feelings,
I can relate to others,
even help them.

And hearing:
I can hear the sound of music
and the song of birds
and human voices.

And sight:
I can look at flowers
and trees
and stars at night
and the faces of my friends.

I am full of gratitude for taste
and smell
and touch,
for thought
and memory
and fantasy
and feeling.

And now the time has come
to be grateful for paralysis itself:

I look at the blessings it has brought
till I can see it as a gift.
If I can bring myself to do this
I will have tasted
a moment of the purest mysticism,
namely, of an acceptance of everything that is.

I now reflect on something in my life
that I resent,
resist:
a physical defect,
an illness,
an unavoidable situation,
a circumstance I live in,
a happening of the past,
a person.

And, step by step,
I do with it what I did with my "paralysis."
So that, without relinquishing
my desire and my efforts
to get rid of it if possible,
I bring myself to gratitude for it,
for everything,
for every single thing.

THE MIRAGE

I walk into a desert where the sand and sky
stretch out into infinity
and I am all alone.

Solitude is an act of love, a kindness to myself.
Nothing here distracts me from myself,
so I give my time to thinking of
and speaking to myself
in a positive, friendly kind of way.

Solitude brings perspective:

There were people on the earth
three thousand years ago
whose problems were as big as mine
—or even bigger.
I get into those times in fantasy and see them.

Where are those people now?
I search for what remains of them.

I come to earth three thousand years from now.
The old familiar places

are invaded by the desert or the jungle
or by a people whose language, food, and living habits
are completely foreign to me.
The very names of my hometown and my country
have been changed!
I stand on the spot I am on now
—if I can find it—
and look back on my problems
of three thousand years ago!

Solitude gives distance.
Distance brings serenity
with which to see what lies in store for me today
before I leave the desert.

THE RIVER

I look up at the sky and see the morning star
burn brightly in the heavens.
I imagine what it sees as it looks down
on me and my surroundings
and this portion of the earth.

I visualize what it must have seen
a thousand years ago today . . .
five thousand . . .
a hundred thousand . . .
five million years ago.

I attempt to see in fantasy
what the morning star will see
a thousand years . . .
five thousand . . .
a hundred thousand . . .
five million years from now
on the anniversary of this day.

I pass in review the various stages of my life—
infancy, childhood, adolescence,
adulthood, middle age—
in the following fashion:

I search for the things
that seemed immeasurably important

at each of these stages of my life,
things that caused me worry and anxiety,
things that I stubbornly clung to,
that I thought I could never live with
or without.

When I look back from the distance of today,
how many of those loves and dreams and fears
retain the hold they had on me in former years?

Then I review
some of the problems that I have today,
some of my present sufferings,
and of each of them I say,
"This too will pass away."

I think of things I cling to
or that I am possessive of.
I realize that a day must surely come
when I shall see them differently.
So of each of these attachments too I say,
"This too will pass away."

I make a list of the many things I fear,
and of each of them I say,
"This too will pass away."

To end, I see myself embarking on my daily tasks
with the earnestness
and fervor
with which I plunge into a drama
or a game,
absorbed, immersed, but never drowning.

126

THE ESSENCE

Thousands of persons have died
everywhere in the world
in the past twenty-four hours.
I imagine some of those deaths
—the violent ones . . . the peaceful ones.
The light of life still burns in me.
For how much longer would I like to have it burn?

If I could choose the circumstances of my death,
what would I choose?
What place?
What time of day?
What season of the year?
Would I like to die awake or in my sleep?
To die alone or have the company of people?
What people?
What kind of thoughts, what kind of words
would I want to have in me when I am dying?

I list the things
that I am going to miss the most in death.
Not just sublime and lofty things
like love and beauty,
but little things like the smell of fresh-baked bread,
the patter of the rain,

the rough feel of a blanket,
the taste of coffee,
my favorite magazine.

I call to mind a host of things like these,
with love and gratitude.

And I think how many of them
I am likely to experience
in the days ahead.

When my life is coming to an end,
how many experiences shall I look back to and say,
"To have experienced that alone
would have made my life worthwhile"?

And of how many of my actions shall I say,
"To have done this thing alone
would have made my life worth living"?

I relive and relish
these experiences and actions.

I finally turn to God to express to him,
in silence or in words,
what is uppermost in my heart.

THE GOOD NEWS

I imagine that I have a few days left of life.
I am allowed to choose just one person,
or at the most two,
to be with me for these last days.
I make the painful choice,
then I talk with this person,
explaining why it is I chose him or her.

I am allowed to have
a three-minute conversation on the phone
with any persons of my choice
or to send each one of them a written message.
Whom do I choose?
What do I say?
What does each of them reply?

I have a final chance
to reach out to people I disliked
or people I ignored.
If I take it, what do I say to each of them
now that I feel myself to be
on the threshold of eternity?

People ask me if I have a final wish.
Have I?

A friend tells me he plans to speak
at my memorial service.
I suggest a point or two
for him to put into his speech.

One day, alone in my room,
I think of the things in my life
I am especially thankful for,
the things that I am proud of.

Then I turn to the things I regret
and wish had never happened,
especially my sins.

While I am thus engaged, Jesus Christ walks in.
His presence brings the sweetest joy and peace.
I tell him some of the things about my life that I regret.
He stops me with the words,
"That is all forgiven and forgotten.
Do you not know
that love keeps no record of wrongs?" (1 Cor. 13:5).
Then he goes on to say,
"In fact, your wrongs have not just been forgiven.
They have even been converted into grace.
Have you never been told
that where the sin was great,
grace was greater still?" (Rom. 5:21).

This seems too good to be true
for my poor fearful heart!
Then I hear him say, "I am so pleased with you,
so grateful to you."
I begin to protest that there is nothing in my life
that he can be so pleased about or grateful for.
He says, "Surely you would be grateful beyond words
to anyone who did for you
even a small part of what you did for me?
Do you think I have less of a heart than you?"

So I lean back
and allow the impact of his words to hit me,
rejoicing in my heart
that I have such a God as he.

THE DELIVERANCE

To see life as it truly is, nothing helps so much
as the reality of death.

I imagine I am present at my funeral.
I see my body in the coffin,
I smell the flowers and incense,
I witness every detail of the funeral rites.

My eyes rest briefly on each person present at the funeral.
Now I understand
how short a time they have to live themselves,
only they are not aware of it.
Right now their mind is focused,
not on their own death or the shortness of their life,
but on me.
This is my show today—my last great show on earth,
the last time I shall be the center of attention.

I listen to what the priest is saying about me in his homily.
And as I scan the faces of the congregation
it gives me pleasure to observe that I am missed.
I leave a vacuum in the hearts and lives of friends.
It is also sobering to think
that there may be people in that crowd
who are pleased that I am gone.

I walk in the procession to the graveyard.
I see the group stand silent at the grave

while the final prayers are said.
I see the coffin sink into the grave
—the final chapter of my life.

I think what a good life it was,
with all its ups and downs,
its periods of excitement and monotony,
its achievements and frustrations.
I stay on beside the grave
recalling chapters of my life
as the people in the crowd go back
to their homes, their daily chores,
their dreams and worries.

A year goes by and I return to earth.
The painful vacuums I left behind
are steadily being filled:
the memory of me survives in the hearts of friends,
but they think about me less.
They now look forward to other people's letters,
they relax in other people's company;
other people have become important in their lives.
And so it must be: life must go on.

I visit the scene of my work.
If it still continues, someone else is doing it,
someone else is making the decisions.

The places I used to frequent only a year ago:
the shops, the streets, the restaurants . . .
they are all there.
And it doesn't seem to matter that I walked those streets
and visited those shops and rode those buses.
I am not missed. Not there!

I search for personal effects like my watch, my pen,
and those possessions that had sentimental value for me:
souvenirs, letters, photographs.
And the furniture I used, my clothes, my books.

I return on the fiftieth anniversary of my death
and look around to see
if someone still remembers me or speaks of me.

A hundred years go by and I come back again.
Except for a faded photograph or two in an album or on a wall
and the inscription on my grave, little is left of me.
Not even the memory of friends, because none of them exists.
Still, I search for any traces
that are possibly left on earth of my existence.

I look into my grave to find a handful of dust
and crumbling bones in my coffin.
I rest my eyes on that dust
and think back on my life—
the triumphs, the tragedies,
the anxieties and the joys,
the strivings, the conflicts,
the ambitions, the dreams,
the loves and the repugnances
that constituted my existence
—all of it scattered to the winds,
absorbed into the universe.
Only a little dust remains to indicate that it ever was,
that life of mine!

As I contemplate that dust
it is as if a mighty weight is lifted from my shoulders
—the weight that comes from thinking that I matter.

Then I look up and contemplate the world around me
—the trees, the birds, the earth,
the stars, the sunshine,
a baby's cry, a rushing train, the hurrying crowds,
the dance of life and of the universe—
and I know that somewhere in all of these
are the remains of that person I called me
and that life that I called mine.

THE SYMPHONY

I return to meditate on death,
the better to get a feel for the mystery of life.
I imagine a village graveyard lined with trees
where my body has recently been buried.

I sit beside my grave
and picture my body as vividly as possible.
It is as if I touch each limb
and feel its coldness and rigidity.

I do this for a while, then take a look at nature.
It is dark, just before the break of dawn.
I look at the horizon till the blackness starts to melt.

The village cocks begin to crow,
people stir about as lamps are lit.
The silence of the dawn is somehow heightened
by these sounds of life awaking.

I once again see through my coffin
with the eyes of fantasy.
My body is a sickly blue.
I look at it from head to toe
taking care that no part is omitted.

The dawn illumines the horizon.
The clouds are tinged with color.
The morning star shines single and serene.

I listen to the village sounds
and imagine what is happening there.

Back to my body:
I look on as the skin begins to break
—the sign of putrefaction.

It is midmorning.
The clouds are white, the sky is blue,
the trees are a bright and shiny green.
The breeze stirs up a murmur in the leaves.

Children's voices fill the air
as they recite their lessons
or run around in play.
The men are in the fields,
the women in their kitchens.
The bustle of life!

Partial decomposition has begun,
disfiguring my face, my chest, my stomach.
I have to force myself to look.

I hurriedly return to nature
and see that it is noon.
The sun is at its zenith.
I hear the buzz of bugs and bees.

The village quiets down:
it is time for lunch and rest.

Total decomposition has set in all over my body:
my scalp, my head, my face, my chest,
shoulders, arms, hands, stomach,
genitals, thighs, legs, toes . . .
one huge mass of putrefaction.

The atmosphere is thick and lazy with the heat.
I see the play of light and shadow on the ground.
Nature seems to hold her breath in the sultry afternoon.

Not a sound comes from the village.

The decomposition is mostly over now.
A skeleton emerges
through the chunks of flesh that still cling on to it.
I recall the shape of the body
that once filled out that skeleton.

It is evening.
I hear the lowing of the cattle
as they come home from the pasture.
I am strangely moved by the striking of the temple gong
and enraptured by the sunset.

The village lamps are lit.
An evening breeze blows through the cemetery.
The stars begin to twinkle.

When I next look at my body I see nothing but a skeleton.
I rest my eyes on every one
of those clean white bones.

Around me it is night,
suppertime in the village.
People sit around the fire, talking:
the occasional sound of an argument drifts through the air.

The moonlight filters through the trees.

The skeleton in my grave has broken up
into disjointed bones, disintegrating.
I gaze at each one separately.

It is midnight.
The breeze has died down . . . all is still . . .
the moon holds sway over the night.

The lights have gone out in the village.

One final look at my grave:
that empty coffin once contained a body
that seems to have stealthily crept away,
leaving only dust behind.

It is early morning.
Nature's waking sounds are all around me.
The trees begin to clothe themselves in freshness.

The villagers prepare to move into another day.

I hear a bird sing on a nearby tree.
I wonder what it sings of.
It has a special quality, this birdsong in a cemetery!

I listen to the song
and contemplate my body turned to dust
and watch the dance of life go on around me.

THE DISPENSATION

I imagine I am told I have six weeks more to live.
I see the circumstances vividly:
How old I am . . .
and where . . .
what I am dying of.

I go through the pain of saying goodbye to life
and to each of the things that I loved
and hated.

> I do this through a dialogue
> in which these things
> —and life—
> talk back to me.

I notice the reactions of people to the news
that I am going to die.
I think what each of them is going to lose
in losing me.

After death I stand before the Lord.
I talk to him about my life:
the things that pleased me most
and the things I most regret.

Now I hear God say
that he plans to send me back to life.
He leaves me free to choose
the form of my reincarnation:

What country do I choose?

What sex?

What kind of person would I want to be?
I choose my temperament
and talents,
my virtues and defects,
the experiences I want to have in my new life.

What social stratum do I wish to be born in
—rich, middle class, poor?
Why?

What kind of parents do I choose?
I select the qualities and defects
I wish each of them to have.
I imagine that I say this to my present parents
and see how they react.

What kind of childhood would I want to have?
How many siblings?

What kind of education?

What do I choose for my life's work?

I listen now as God explains why he chose for me
the life I have at present
in each of its details.

THE COMEDY

I travel to a solitary mountaintop
and have a whole day to myself.
What topics . . .
aspects of my life . . .
persons . . .
do I choose to think of
now that I have the leisure?

I do this for some time
in a way that will be fruitful.

How many names can I recall
of persons who excelled two thousand . . .
five . . . ten thousand years ago?

I picture scenes of life in ancient Greece . . .
or Rome . . . or Egypt . . .
India . . . China . . . the Americas . . .
love affairs and wars,
births and deaths,
dynasties and revolutions,
rites and superstitions,
the daily lives of ordinary folk.
And then I see how time erodes
all memory of these peoples
and their cultures.

I now decide which outstanding persons,
which events, of our own day
will find a place in history books
ten thousand years from now.
And what effect my own existence
will have had on human history
at that time.

I travel into outer space till earth becomes
a brightly colored tennis ball afloat in space,
revolving on its axis.
I merely gaze at it for as long a time as possible,
for the sight will do me good.
I search for the cities, rivers, airports, churches,
the wars, the celebrations,
the loves and hates
on the surface of that tiny globe.

Then I search for me and my achievements
till I see myself cut down to proper size
and experience the relief that distance brings,
till I can laugh wholeheartedly again
—for laughter, especially at oneself,
is the blessed gift of solitude!

Before I come down from the mountaintop
to my everyday routine
I ask myself, "What do I want to make of my existence
here on earth?"
And also, "How do I want to live my life today?"
And I open my mind to what suggests itself to me.

THE CYCLE

In the middle of a desert
stands the temple of a lost religion.
I inspect the ruins carefully
and fantasize:

I see the city where the temple stood.
Who built the temple? For what purpose?
I see the plans,
the architect,
the builders,
the quarry for the temple stones,
the sources where the money came from
—and I observe the feelings
of the builders and the people
as the temple nears completion.

I imagine I am there the day the temple is anointed,
the god installed:
I am in the midst of the procession, the music,
the chanting, the rites of consecration,
and I look into the eyes and hearts
of the people at the ceremony.

One day I sit inside the temple
unobserved, observing:
someone comes there in deep distress.

I see what goes on in his heart
and the result of his devotions.

Another comes for meditation.
He is a seeker after God and peace
and the meaning of existence.
What method does he follow in his seeking?

Here comes another who is in love with God.
What could have caused this?
How does she express her love?

I see the never-ending line of devotees
who come to ask for favors,
to seek protection from every sort of evil.

I see the priests: what kind of men they are,
what kind of lives they live,
their convictions and beliefs.

I take a final look at the temple
when it is at its zenith:
when the temple gong sounds a call to pray
throughout the neighboring countryside,
when frequent offerings are made
to the temple's deity
and the priests perform the sacred rites each day.

But the day inexorably comes when decay sets in.
What happens?
Are the people converted to another religion?
Do pestilence and famine hit the land,
forcing people to migrate?

I see the temple go through stages of neglect
till there are no more devotees and priests,
till there is no one living in the neighborhood
and the sun, the wind, the rain
play havoc on the building.

I talk to the dilapidated temple.
And as I listen to the ancient temple's words
my heart grows wiser,
for it gains a deeper knowledge
of life
and death
and God
and history
and human beings.

I finally ask the temple
for a special word of wisdom
to take away with me.

Then I say goodbye
and walk away.

THE EXPEDITION

My retreat has come to an end,
and I think of the days that I have spent
in these surroundings.

I see an image of myself as I was when I came here
and I look at myself as I am today
at the close of the retreat.

I think of the persons and places
that have been a part of my retreat.
To each of them I speak in gratitude
and to each I say goodbye:
other places, other persons call to me
and I must go.

I think of the experiences I have had,
the graces I have been granted
in this place.
For each of these too I am grateful.

I think of the kind of life I have lived here,
the atmosphere, the daily schedule,
I say goodbye to them:
another type of life awaits me,
other graces, other experiences.

And as I say goodbye to persons,
places,
things,

events,
experiences,
and graces,
I do so under life's imperious bidding:
if I wish to be alive
I must learn to die at every moment,
that is, to say goodbye, let go, move on.

When this is done, I turn to face the future
and I say, "Welcome."

I imagine my trip from this place tomorrow
and I say, "Welcome."

I think of the work that waits for me,
the people I shall meet,
the type of life I shall be living,
the events that will take place tomorrow.
And I extend my arms in welcome
to the summons of the future.

THE ECSTASY

I attempt to look at life in all its richness,
seeking to be affected
at levels deeper than those of thought.

For this I contemplate contrasting scenes:

The birth of a baby—
the parent's joy and sense of wonder,
the celebrations.
Then I contemplate a death—
the grief, the sense of loss,
the funeral rites.
I move repeatedly from one scene to the other,
observing every detail.

The next pair: a wedding hall and a cancer ward.
Again I notice each detail
as I contemplate the scenes.
I move from one scene to the other,
from the wedding to the ward and back again,
avoiding all reflection,
content to merely look.

Then a sports stadium
—the crowds, the players,
the cheering, the excitement.
And an old folks' home
—an elderly person sitting at a window
reminiscing.

I move from one scene to the other,
looking into the hearts
of the persons in the scenes.

Next I see the swimming pool of a luxury hotel
—the sparkling water,
the sounds of merriment,
the bright sun in the sky.
And the slums of the poor
—the fetid atmosphere, the stench,
the people sleeping on the ground,
the rats and cockroaches.
I make no reflections.
I merely get into the mood
of the scene I contemplate.

I watch a cabinet meeting in progress:
the powerful of the land making decisions
that will affect the lives of other people.
And I contrast this with a torture chamber
that I examine in detail.

Then I step back from earth and see these
and an infinity of other scenes together
and, though I cannot understand it,
I see the whole of it as forming one symphony,
one harmonious dance:
birth and death,
laughter and tears,
pleasure and pain,
virtue and vice
—all blending to form a fresco
of incomparable beauty,
quite beyond the comprehension of my thinking mind.

Then I return to the christening and the funeral,
the wedding and the cancer ward,
the stadium and the old folks home,
and I see them as separate notes of the same melody,
different movements of a single dance.

I see Jesus Christ and Judas,
I see victims and persecutors,
the killers and the crucified:
one melody in the contrasting notes,
one dance moving through different steps.

I think of the people who dislike me and attack me
and I see them and me as different,
yet not-two,
engaged in one task,
one dance,
one work of art.
I contemplate the variedness of my own life
with its changing moods, its ups and downs . . .
and the people who touch my life,
the evil and the good,
the loved and the unloved . . .
many movements of a single dance
performed by a single dancer.

Finally, I stand before the Lord.
I see him as the dancer
and all of this maddening,
senseless,
exhilarating,
agonizing,
splendorous thing

that we call life
as his dance.

And I stand speechless,
uncomprehending,
lost in wonder!

LOVE

THE SANCTUARY

I make my way into the temple of my heart
and invent a form of worship
that seems accordant with the time of day
or with my present mood.

Enshrined there in the temple
are the persons who have changed me
by their love . . .

And those whom I have changed by mine.

At the end of my devotions
I place my hands on each of them
to share with them
the grace God gave me in my worship.

To how many of these persons can I say,
"I am certain that your love for me
will last forever?"

To how many can I say,
"You can be sure my love for you
will never die?"

I choose a person
of whose love I am completely certain.

I go back to the times
when I felt this person's love,
relive those times in fantasy,
allow myself to feel the joy they bring,
and stay with it for as long a time as possible,
for in doing so I drink in love
—and life
and God.

I now come to the present
and see this person,
living or dead it matters not,
sitting here before me.
We hold hands.
I let his or her love flow into me
and imagine I am energized by it.

I let my own love flow into this person.
The two love currents flow into each other
and generate an atmosphere of love around us.

And so I end this exercise
as I began it,
in a temple
—for loving is divine and God is love.

THE FOUNTAIN

I attempt to get in touch with my thirst
for happiness,
for peace,
for love,
for truth,
for something quite beyond me, I know not what.

Then I recite the scripture texts that follow
to give expression to this thirst.

The first text is a *cry:*
It says, "Oh God, you are my God,
for you I long.
For you my soul is thirsting" (Psalm 62:1).

> As I repeat each text in the manner of a mantra,
> allowing it to penetrate my heart,
> I focus on one word, one phrase
> within the text
> that seems to call to me above the others.
>
> And I let my mind produce some image
> or some scene (maybe from my own history)
> that would symbolize the text my heart recites.

The second is an *invitation:*
"Anyone who is thirsty

should come to me
and drink" (John 7:37).

The third one is a *promise:*
"Whoever drinks the water that I give
will never thirst again.
The water that I give will be an inner spring
that wells up for eternal life" (John 4:13–14).

The final text is the *fulfilment:*
"The Spirit and the bride say, 'Come!'
Let everyone who listens answer, 'Come!'
Let all those who are thirsty come.
All who want may have the water of life
and have it free. Amen.
Come Lord Jesus" (Rev. 22:17).

THE PARTING

I get the feel of my body . . .
the pleasant and unpleasant sensations in it . . .

I think of the kind of body I shall have
when I am dying . . .
What feelings will I have then for this body
that has grown with me from infancy to death?

I make believe that I am dying . . .
Having taken leave of everyone . . .
I take leave of my body,
filling each part of it
with gratitude and love.

I start off with my hands:
I look at them
and think what they have meant to me.

Hands to pray:
to hold my beads and book of prayers,
to touch in veneration.
Hands that came together to beg
and to adore
and deepen concentration.
Would I have been less fervent
if I had had no hands to pray with?

160

Hands for loving:
countless scenes pass through my mind
of times when, through my hands,
my love went out to people
—to caress and to console,
to hold . . . protect . . .
encourage . . . understand.
Would I have loved creation less
without my hands to help me?

Hands for service:
to wash and nurse and carry loads.
But for these hands I would have been excluded
from a thousand forms of service.

Hands for creativity:
for gardening and cooking,
for painting, decorating, making music.
Without my hands would life have been less joyful?

Hands for survival:
how constantly I used them
to feed and clothe and wash and heal myself,
to stop myself from falling, ward off danger,
to reach into the environment and satisfy my needs.

I see the role my hands have had in forming me
and I am filled with gratitude to them.

Then I do the same for every other sense
and limb
and organ of my body.

THE EDUCATION

The gospels tell how Jesus turned
and looked at Peter
—and how that look changed Peter's heart (Matt. 26:75).

If Jesus were to come back to the world today,
what would he look at first?

I imagine that what first attracts his notice
is the overwhelming goodness in humanity.
The good-hearted person sees goodness everywhere;
the evil-hearted evil,
for we tend to see in others
the reflection of ourselves.

Jesus uncovers by his look
the love, the honesty, and goodness
that hides in every human being.

I see him looking at a prostitute,
then I look at her as he does
to discover what he sees in her.
I see him look at hardened tax-collectors,
at an adulterous woman,
at a thief on a cross beside him,
and I learn the art of looking!

When Jesus looks at evil he calls it by its name
and condemns it unambiguously.
Only, where I see malice,
he sees ignorance.
At the moment of his death
I see him drop his anger at the Pharisees;
he looks beyond their seeming malice:
"Father, forgive them,
for they do not know what they are doing."
I take my time to look and listen,
for it will educate my heart.

I now look at the world myself.
I imagine that each time I meet a stranger
or walk into a group of people
I see each person's goodness.

I look at all the people I live
and work with.
How much goodness can I see
in each of them?

It is impossible for me to love "evil" people
and people I dislike
unless, like Jesus, I see good in them.
So I imagine Jesus here beside me
teaching me to look at them afresh:
to make allowances,
to search for ignorance
and mitigating circumstances.

After which I say something like this
to each of them:
"Your deeds are evil, true, but you are good."
Or I say, "I condemn the evil you are doing,

but I cannot censure you,
for you really do not know what you are doing."

To end this exercise I expose myself
to the loving look of Jesus.
As I gaze into his eyes I am amazed
at the goodness he detects in me.
I tend to blame myself for all the wrong I do
—he uncompromisingly condemns my sin,
but stubbornly refuses to condemn the sinner.

I shrink, at first, from his loving gaze,
for it is too forgiving
and, in my hatred of myself, I cannot bear it.
But I know I must sustain that look
if I am to learn to look at other people
the way he looks at me.

THE CURRENT

I pray to God that he will use
me as a channel of his love and peace.

Then I compose a mantra
that would formulate this prayer of mine
—something like, "Make me a channel of your peace."

I recite the mantra for a while,
linking it with the rhythm of my pulse
or breathing.

The two things that most prevent me
from being a channel of God's grace
are noise and sin.

So I begin by seeking silence
as an antidote to noise:
I silence all my thinking
and all interior speech,
the mantra not excluded,
by becoming conscious of my breathing
or the sensations of my body.

Then I seek to cleanse my heart of sin:
I place before the Lord my feelings of resentment,
anger, greed, possessiveness, and jealousy,
even mild dislikes and irritations,

asking him to cleanse my heart of them
so that his grace will flow through me unhampered.

Having attained a respite
from my noise and negativity
I imagine that a stream of love and peace
wells up in me,
flooding my being,
then moving out.

First I guide it in the direction
of people who are dear to me.

Then I direct the flow
to those whom I shall meet today.

Now I unleash the current
onto people who oppose me
or dislike me
and those whom I dislike.

Finally I let it flow abundant, indiscriminate,
to every creature in the universe:
to animals and birds and trees
and things inanimate.

THE SUNRISE

I become aware of all the sounds around me,
of my surroundings: the grounds, the trees,
this room, the furniture;
then of my body
and my breathing.

Now each time I exhale
I pronounce the name of Jesus
slowly, peacefully.

I imagine that despite the brightness of the sun
there is a darkness
at the heart of every being
that only grace can banish.

To exterminate the darkness
I pronounce the name over each part of my being
that is in need of healing
(my heart . . . my mind . . . my limbs . . . my
senses . . .)
and I see each part become aglow,
alive with grace.

Then I create an atmosphere of grace
in which to live and move and have my being:

I begin with the walls
and furniture of my room,
making them luminous with the name.
Then everything I shall use today:
my books and pen,
my clothes, my shoes.
The house: the dining room, its furniture,
the cutlery, the crockery,
the kitchen, its utensils,
the food I eat,
the water I shall drink and wash in.
The grounds, the trees, the birds . . .
all grace-filled and illumined by the name.

I now pronounce his name
over every person I shall meet today
and see them glow with health and grace.

I finally recite the name over the earth
and all its peoples . . .
the sun, the moon, the universe
and the whole wide immensity of space.

THE ANOINTING

My retreat comes to an end today.
Having said my goodbyes
I come into the sanctuary of my heart
to seek the blessing of the Lord before I leave.

I sit down at his feet
and silently recite his name.
I pay attention to the sentiments that fill my heart
and to what it is I am really saying to him
when I recite his name.

Then I anoint myself and every part of me
—spirit, heart, mind, and body—
through the recitation of his name.

I review these days of my retreat
—the persons, the places, the events, the things
that have been part of my experience,
and I gratefully breathe the name on each of them.

The places: my favorite spots on the grounds
and in the neighborhood . . .
I fill them with his grace
that other people coming to these places will be blessed.

I anoint my room and furniture,
filling them with grace for future occupants.

I do the same to other places of the house:
the dining room, the kitchen,
the chapel, the corridors,
the library, the showers.

I do this for the trees on the grounds
so that all who seek their shade
will also have divine protection,
and for the birds,
that their songs will do for others
what they have done for me.

And those experiences I was given
—the insights, the grace-filled moments:
I anoint them too to make them fruitful.

I anoint the persons
who have been a part of my experience here.

Then I look into the future:
events that are likely to occur,
actions I shall perform,
people I am going to meet,
I make them holy with the ointment of the name,
sending it on ahead of me,
so that everywhere I go
I shall be protected and fortified
and made alive.

THE BENEDICTION

Today I choose to pray for others.
But how shall I impart to them
the gift of peace and love
if my own heart is still unloving
and I have no peace of mind myself?

So I start with my heart:
I hold before the Lord
each feeling of resentment, anger, bitterness
that may still be lurking there,
asking that his grace
will make it yield to love someday
if not right now.

Then I seek peace:
I list the worries that disturb my peace of mind
and imagine that I place them in God's hands
in the hope that this will bring me respite from anxiety
at least during this time of prayer.

Then I seek the depth that silence brings,
for prayer that springs from silence
is powerful and effective.
So I listen to the sounds around me
or become aware of the feelings
and sensations in my body
or my breathing in and out.

First I pray for people whom I love.
Over each of them I say a blessing:
"May you be safe from harm and evil,"
imagining that my words create
a protective shield of grace around them.

Then I move on to people I dislike
and people who dislike me.
Over each of them I say this prayer:
"May you and I be friends some day,"
imagining some future scene
where this comes to pass.

I think of anxious people whom I know,
people who are depressed.
To each of them I say:
"May you find peace and joy,"
imagining that my wish for them becomes reality.

I think of people who are handicapped,
people who are in pain, and say:
"May you find strength and courage,"
imagining that my words unleash resources
within each of them.

I think of lonely people:
people lacking love
or separated from their loved ones,
and to each of them I say:
"May God's abiding company be yours."

I think of older people who,
with the passing of each day,
must face the reality of approaching death,
and to each of them I say:
"May you find the grace to joyfully let go of life."

I think of the young and recite this prayer:
"May the promise of your youth be met
and your life be fruitful."

Finally I say to each of the people I live with:
"May my contact with you be a grace for both of us."

I come back to my heart now to rest awhile
in the silence that I find there
and in the loving feeling
that has come alive in me
as a consequence of my prayer for others.

THE CELEBRATION

As a preparation for this exercise
I read Matthew 26:26–30
Luke 22:14–19
and John 13–17

I imagine I hear Jesus say, "Prepare a place for me,
for I am going to dine with you tonight."
I choose a place.
Whom do I invite to this unusual supper?
What preparations do my friends and I make for it?

The time has finally arrived.
I see the room, the food,
the bread and wine,
the friends I have invited.

When introducing Jesus to my friends
I invent an adjective for each of them.
For instance, "This is John, the Faithful;
this is Ann, the Loving;
this is Gentle Joseph."

Then Jesus gives a sign of love to each of us
and the meal begins.

Quite early in the meal Jesus breaks a loaf of bread
and comes around to offer it to each of us.
To each he says a sentence.
What does he say to me?

After the bread is eaten the meal goes on.
Jesus often speaks,
sometimes in answer to our questions,
sometimes unasked.

He speaks of love.
It is as if he spoke to me alone.

He tells us of discipleship
and the persecution that must go with it.
We ask him what this means concretely in our lives.

He then goes on to talk of peace.
And I ask myself how much I have of it,
what obstacles I put to it.

He talks about a joy
that comes from his mysterious presence
that no one can deprive us of,
so we question him about this joy,
this "presence,"
and I recall the moments when I felt it in my life.

We know this meal is linked
in some mysterious way
to his and our existence:
to passion, death, and resurrection.
So we talk with him about this too.

Supper is almost over.
Jesus pronounces sacred words

over a glass of wine
and offers it to each of us.
Again he says a sentence as he offers it.
What does he say to me?

After the wine is drunk, silence invades the room.
Then Jesus prays aloud for me and for my friends.
I hear him pray that we will be united,
that we will foster unity wherever we may be.

It is time for us to leave.
We stand as Jesus leads us in a song of praise.
And as I sing, I savor in my heart
the sentiments created by this supper I prepared
for Jesus and my friends.

THE PILGRIM

I dwell on the feelings and associations
that the word "home" evokes in me.
I relive some events
connected with my childhood and my home
—the times of joy and freedom,
the times, maybe, of fear and sadness.

I imagine the kind of home mine would have been
if I had married:
the kind of spouse I would have had . . .
and been . . .
how many children we would have had,
the names we would have given each of them,
the sort of house we would have lived in
and the atmosphere we would have given it.

I now reflect that home is where my heart is.
Where is my heart today?
In what person, place or occupation?
If God gave me the power
to be anywhere on earth right now,
where would I go?

I imagine that I go there now
and explain to this particular "home" of mine
what it is that draws me to it.

I probably have more than one home.
So I talk with each of them in the same way.

I return to my dream home now
and talk to the spouse I shall never marry,
explaining why.
I talk to my first-born child,
who will never know existence
and never nestle in my arms,
explaining why it must be so.

I also talk with my dream home,
and am aware of my feelings as I say goodbye to it
and to my spouse and children,
taking responsibility for the fact
that they will never be.

Then I return to each of those homes
my heart would fly to if it could,
and I see how each can be a prison,
an enemy to freedom, life, and growth,
a cozy nest, luring me to settle down
rather than use my wings and fly.

So I lovingly explain to each
that I may not stay, I may not rest,
for I have promises to keep.

I see myself in fantasy
on the road that leads from home to new horizons.
And I discover to my joy
that the Lord is here beside me on the road,
showing me that if I wish to be alive and free

I must shed my fear of walking unaccompanied;
then he will be my constant resting place,
for everywhere I go he will be present
—and then, at last, the whole of creation
will be a home to me.

We come to a rise in the road, the Lord and I.
I turn back to take a final look at my home
there in the distance
—and my heart wells up with gratitude and love
at the sight of that nest
where destiny decreed that I should stay
till I built up strength to fly.

THE REUNION

I imagine I am given the whole of today
to spend in solitude on a mountaintop
and observe how I react to this.

Solitude is togetherness:
it is here I get together with myself,
with all creation
and with being.
Apart from solitude I am scattered and fragmented.

So on the mountaintop I start with me:
I become affectionately conscious of my body:
its posture,
its state of well-being or discomfort,
its present mood.

My awareness rests on every part of me:
each limb,
each sense,
each organ,
my breathing in and out
and the working of my lungs,
my heart
and blood
and brain
and every other function:
my seeing,

hearing,
tasting,
smelling,
touching,
thinking,
willing,
reminiscing,
feeling.

Before I come down from the mountaintop
I look at all creation and draw it to my heart.

I love the birds and animals . . .
the trees . . . the sun . . .
the air . . . the clouds . . . the grass . . .
the mountains . . . rivers . . . seas . . .
and earth and stars and universe.

I love the room I live in
and the furniture I use,
the kitchen and the fire and the food.
I love the cooling water I shall drink
and splash upon my face.

I love the distant traffic . . .
the roads . . . the fields . . . the factories . . .
the homes . . . the theaters, shops, and restaurants.

I love the people I shall meet today
and press each person to my heart,
and I love all peoples everywhere
in every corner of the globe,

and peoples of the past,
and those of future centuries,
for in solitude I acquire the awareness
and the depth to do this.

SILENCE

THE TREASURE

Recite the name interiorly.

What are you saying to the Lord
through the recitation of his name?

Imagine you are weak
and the name becomes a tonic
that strengthens you.
You feel the tonic's power increase
each time you say the name.

There is a darkness all around you
and within . . .
and the name dispels the darkness.
Within, you become luminous;
outside, it is as if the name lights up your path.

Imagine that the name becomes a shield about you,
dispelling every evil,
and protecting you from harm.

THE FUSION

You descend to the depths of your being
to find a mantra there, a word
recited to the rhythm of your heartbeats.
It is the expression of your longing and your love.

At first you hear it dimly,
but it gradually grows louder.

Now listen to the word
resounding in the whole of you . . .
your heart, your head,
your limbs, your stomach.

Do not pronounce the word.
Only listen,
rejoicing in the thought
that while it resounds in you
it makes you whole.

Now see it break through
the barriers of your being
and invade the world around you
—the earth and sky
and all the universe.

You are the center from which it ripples out
to the frontiers of the world.

See every creature throb
to the rhythm of your heartbeat
and of your hidden word.
Plants and birds and stones
and trees and stars and sun
resound with the word
and by it are made whole.

Now melt into the word,
becoming one with it,
and shout it out interiorly
with all your strength.

THE CARESS

Become aware of each sensation
on the surface of your skin,
beginning with the crown of your head
and moving downward to the tip of your toes.

It matters not that you feel no sensation
in some parts of your body.
The mere attempt to feel them
will give you the benefit of this exercise.

Now reflect that each sensation
is a biochemical reaction
that needs God's almighty power to exist.

Imagine you experience God's power
each time you experience these sensations.

Imagine each sensation to be a touch of God—
rough, smooth, pleasurable, painful.

Imagine this touch of God to be luminous
and healing.

THE OCEAN

Focus on your breathing.
Be aware of the *fact* that you are breathing in
and breathing out.

Now focus on the flow of the air
through your nostrils
the way you would if you were watching
the ebb and flow of the sea.

Where do you feel the touch of the air
in your nostrils
as you breathe in?

Where as you breathe out?

Is the volume of air passing through one nostril
greater than that passing through the other?

Observe the difference of temperature in the air
as it goes in and comes out.

Now use imagery that will affect you
at deeper, more subconscious, levels.

Imagine the outgoing air to be a polluted stream,
carrying with it your impurities.
Do not focus on any sins in particular
—just your selfishness
and your fearfulness in general.

Fill your lungs with air,
the better to eject these impurities from your heart
when you breathe out.

Now switch your attention to your inhalation:
imagine the atmosphere to be charged
with God's presence.
Fill your lungs
with the life-giving, energizing presence of God.

And as you do this imagine that the whole of you
becomes energized and radiant.

THE GUEST

Close your eyes.
Cover them with the palms of your hands
and simultaneously block your ears with your thumbs.
Listen to the sound of your breathing
for a minute or two.

Now, eyes still closed,
gently lower your hands to rest upon your lap.
Listen to all the sounds around you
—the loud ones and the soft,
the distant and the near.

You will often observe
that what seems at first to be just one sound
is really a combination of many sounds.

Now listen to all those sounds,
not as separate entities
but as forming, all together,
one vast symphony that fills the universe.

Listening to sounds can be as silence-producing
and as fruitful in your search for God
as looking at a river.

You may now give a devotional turn to the exercise
by imagining that you make God the loan of your ears

so that he, who has no ears,
can listen to the harmony
that he produces in creation.

Rest in the thought
of God listening through your ears.

Then open your eyes and rest in the thought
of God looking, through them,
at the beauty of his creation.

THE SURRENDER

Begin by seeking silence.

For this, come home to yourself.
Come to the present.
Ask yourself: Where am I right now?
What am I doing?
What am I thinking?
What am I sensing in my body?
What is the quality of my breathing?

Silence cannot be induced or sought directly.
Just seek awareness—and silence will appear.

If you now wish to communicate with God
within this silence
imagine that you surrender, let go,
each time you breathe out
—that each exhalation
is your way of saying yes to God.
Yes to what you are today
—to the kind of person God has made you,
the kind of person you have become.
Yes to the whole of your past.
Yes to what lies in store for you in future.

Let go each time you breathe out
with the awareness that all will be well.

Let all anxieties cease,
and let peace take over,
for in his hands, in his will,
is our peace.

THE LIGHT

Go over the events of the day
from the moment you woke up
till the present moment.

Start with the first event: waking up.
Look at it from the outside, so to speak,
as a neutral observer would.

Observe
not just the external event of waking up
but your inner reactions: your thoughts
and feelings
and fantasies
and mood.

Then move on to the next event.

And so through every portion of the day.

Do not judge yourself or the event.
Just look.
No condemnation, no approval.
The light of awareness alone

will destroy all that is evil
and bring to life all that is good.

And your life will become luminous
and transparent.

THE GLOW

Turn off the lights in your room
and light a candle.
Place it a few feet away from you.

Now focus on the flame:
sometimes it dances
and you observe its smallest movements,
sometimes it seems motionless and steady.
You may find it more restful to close your eyes
and see the flame in fantasy.

As you look at the flame
think of what it symbolizes for you.
It may be a symbol of many things.

Allow memories of the past
connected with the candle flame
to come to your awareness.

Then conduct a dialogue with the flame
—on life and death, the flame's and yours,
or life and death in general.

Finally put all words and thoughts and memories aside
and contemplate the flame in silence,
thus allowing the flame to give your heart a message,
a wisdom that escapes the grasp of conscious thought.

At the end take leave of the flame
by joining your hands and bowing down to it.
Then respectfully put it out
with the grateful awareness
that it has kindled something in your heart
that you will carry with you through the day.

THE DAWN

Listen to nature waking up to greet the newborn day.

Notice the blending of silence and song in nature:
how varied are creation's songs,
how deep its silence!
None of nature's sounds
disturbs the eternal silence
that enfolds the universe.
If you listen to those sounds
you will some day hear the silence.

What sentiment do you think creation is expressing
as it wakes up,
as it replaces, with activity,
the quiet of the night?

Listen to your heart now.
There is a song there too,
for you are a part of nature.
If you have never heard the song,
you have not really listened.
Listen! What kind of song is it?
Sad . . . happy . . .
hopeful . . . loving?

There is also silence in your heart.
If you become aware

of each thought, each distraction,
each fantasy and feeling,
you cannot fail to sense that silence.

Now see your heart's song blending
with the song of nature all around you.

Listen.
The more sensitive your listening
the more silent you will be.
The more silent you become
the more sensitive will your listening be.

THE WINDOW

Listen to the sound of the rain.

What associations does that sound have for you?
What memories?

Observe the effect of the rain on the trees
as they soak in this blessing from heaven.

Observe its effect on the birds.

See how the earth responds
to this water that stirs up life
in dry and dusty soil.

Look at the leaves:
the fresh young ones springing to life,
the older ones that, but for the rain,
would have stayed a little longer on the trees.

Study the clouds:
where they come from,
where they go.
Follow them on their journey
from their origin to their end.

Look at the raindrops falling on parched earth,
on trees,
on rooftops.
See them in an amorphous state in clouds,

see them take shape and individuality,
then fall to earth to lose themselves.

Look at the raindrops on your window.
They stand apart,
then build a little rivulet
to take in other separate drops
and carry them away.

See the same thing happening
to the clouds
and trees
and leaves
and birds
and animals
and humans
and yourself.

We stand apart,
only to be sucked into the stream of life
and flow away.

THE VISION

Sit on the bank of a river,
in reality or in fantasy,
and watch the water flow.
If you know how to look without reflections
the river will speak,
not to your brain but to your heart,
creating a silence in your spirit,
and a wisdom
that your conscious mind could never grasp.

Or sit in a railway station
and see the crowds go by.
They come within your vision
and disappear, never to be seen again.

Or watch the leaves fall from a tree
and see them decompose and turn to dust.

Light a lamp and look at the flame
the way you looked at the river.
Or light an incense stick
and watch the smoke lose itself in the atmosphere.

Or stand at your window and look at the rain.
Observe the special mood the rain creates in you.
No reflections! Just look, observe, feel.

You see one raindrop stand separate and solitary.
Then it is jerked forward and pulled away.

Only look.
And creation will speak to you
of life and death
and love
and self
and God.

Finally, lie on your back
with arms outstretched
and imagine that you let go
and are carried onward . . .
like the raindrops and the leaves
and the smoke of the incense stick . . .
for you, like them, are a particle of the universe.

So let go . . .
lose yourself . . .
and flow away.

THE MIRROR

The Chinese sage, Lao-tse, says,
"Muddy water, let stand, becomes clear."

Here is an exercise for the stilling of the water,
so the sediment will settle
and things will be seen with clarity.

Become aware of your position in the room,
of your body as a whole,
of each of its members,
and the sensation of each of the members.

Become aware of all the sounds around you.
Keep away from thoughts,
from reflections, however holy,
connected with the sounds,
for they will only stir the muddy water.

Now observe your breathing:
the stream of air
flowing in and out.

Sit on the banks of that stream
and watch it.

Observe, also, the infinitesimal pause
before the air flows in
and the fraction of a space
before the air flows out.

THE SENTINEL

Muddy water becomes clear when still
and reflects the moon at night distinctly.

So still the mind. Stop the thinking process.
Thoughts cannot be stopped directly.
The way to do it is to give the mind
something to focus on.

So focus on your breathing.
Do not control or deepen it.
Only be aware of it.
Be aware of the movement it produces,
no matter how subtle,
in your body,
your lungs,
your diaphragm.

Or be aware of your inhalation
and your exhalation.
To help your attention
you may say interiorly,
"Now I am breathing in,
now I am breathing out."

Become aware of the difference
between the incoming and the outgoing breath:
the difference in duration,
in temperature,
in the smoothness or roughness of the flow.

Make no reflections or considerations.
Just be aware and watch,
the way you watch a river flow
or the motion of the sea
or the passage of a bird across the sky.

As you observe your breathing
you will discover
that no two breaths are similar,
just as no two human faces,
no two sunset skies are quite alike.
If you have not discovered this as yet
your vision is still poor.
When the muddy water settles down
each breath will be
conspicuously different and unique.

Looking at one's breath
can be as fascinating
as looking at a river.
It can still the mind,
and so give rise
to wisdom,
silence,
and a sense of the divine.

Only look
and clarity will follow,
the muddy water will become transparent
—and you will see.

THE RETURN

Begin by coming home to yourself,
becoming present to yourself.

St. Augustine says we must return to self
to make of self
a stepping stone to God.

So come home.
Become aware of where you are right now,
what your posture is,
what you are thinking,
feeling,
sensing.

Do not let a single thought arise
that you are not aware of . . .

Or a single emotion
no matter how elusive.

How many sensations
—subtle, tiny, tenuous,
or gross and large and obvious—
are you able to detect
as you scan your body's surface
from top to toe?

Now become aware
of the sounds around you

and realize that the activity of hearing
is going on,
that the "I" is hearing.

Do the same with your breathing . . .

And with your sensing.

There is no need for any thoughts or sentiments
or any special insights.
Only be aware of the hearing activity of the self
or the sensing activity of the self
or the breathing activity of the self
and you will come home
—back to your self—
and the self will become silent
and God will not be far away.

THE ARRIVAL

Beginning with the crown of your head
and moving downward
till you arrive at the tip of your toes,
become aware of every sensation
on the surface of your skin.

Dwell for a few seconds, no more,
on each part
—your scalp, forehead, eyebrows, eyelids,
cheeks, nose, lips, chin, ears, neck, etc.

If some part seems to yield no sensations,
you may dwell there a little longer
but not for more than half a minute,
after which, whether sensations are discovered there or not,
move on.

If the day should ever come
when you are able to detect sensations
at every single point of the surface of your skin,
know that the time has come
to sharpen your awareness further:
look for "subtler" sensations,
for most of which you will not even have a name.

Then go below your skin
and get the feel of the sensations there
inside your body.

When this too has become accessible to you
return to the exercise of moving downward
from head to toe,
conscious all the while of bodily sensations
—only this time do it rapidly.
Then move upward
from toe to head
—so that the whole cycle is completed
in not more than a minute's time.

Having done this for a stretch of time,
rest in the awareness of your body as a whole
(no consciousness of parts distinct and separate)
alive with millions of sensations.

Rest in this awareness for a long, long time.

THE SELF

Listen to the sounds of Nature,
the better to sense Nature's mood.

Get in touch with her mood,
get into harmony with her,
for she is an extension of yourself
—your wider body.

This is a secret path favored by the mystics
for attaining the loss of self.
So listen
and become attuned.

Now get closer home to self:
become aware of your body
and all its sensations.

Then become aware of your breathing,
the air passing through your nostrils,
the movement of your lungs and diaphragm.

Become conscious of the atmosphere
as it touches the surface of your skin.
Is it hot or cold,
damp or dry?

Now recall the fact that you breathe
not only through your nostrils

but also through every pore.
Magnify each pore a hundred thousand times
and imagine it interacting with the atmosphere.
Imagine the air entering you,
penetrating your body,
while you offer no resistance.

As you observe the surface of your skin
magnified a hundred thousand times over
—molecules of skin interacting
with molecules of air—
ask yourself this question:
"Am I the molecules?
Am I the air?
Am I both?
Who am I?
Who IS I?
WHAT is I?"

Ask yourself this question persistently
in the context of those interacting molecules
and of the mood of Nature all around you.

THE LIBERATION

Become conscious of your body as a whole
and of the sensations you experience
in its various parts.

Now turn your attention
to the one who has been watching
the sensations and the body.

Realize that the observer, the "I,"
is not the same as the sensations
that are being observed.

You may explicitly say to yourself,
"I am not these sensations.
I am not this body."

Now become conscious of your breathing.

Then turn your attention
to the one who has been looking
at the breathing.

Realize that the observer, the "I,"
is different from the breathing
that is being observed.

You may explicitly say to yourself,
"I am not the breathing."

Become conscious of every thought
that you are thinking.
It is quite likely
that soon all thoughts will disappear
and all you will be conscious of is this one thought:
right-now-there-is-no-thinking-in-my-mind.

Turn your attention now
to the one who is attending to those thoughts
or the one who is producing them.

Realize that the observer, the "I,"
is different from the thoughts observed.

You may explicitly say to yourself,
"I am not the thoughts.
I am not the thinking."

Observe a feeling
that you are now experiencing
—or recall one you have had before—
particularly if it is a negative emotion
like fear, anxiety, hurt, discouragement, remorse.

Turn your attention
to the one who has been watching
—or recalling—
the emotion.

Realize that the observer, the "I,"
is different from the feeling
that is being observed.

You may explicitly say to yourself,
"I am not the feeling."

215

SEEDLINGS

If any of the sentences that follow appeals to you, place it in your heart and ponder on its inner meaning. This will cause its inner truth to germinate and grow.

Do not force it open with your mind. That would only kill the seed.

Sow it where the soil is rich. Sow it in your heart. And give it time.

Assent to honor
and acclaim
and you will lose
your freedom.
                    The King

Jesus Christ
and Judas
are movements
of a single dance.
                    The Ecstasy

X The marketplace
is as good a place
for silence
as the monastery,
for silence
is the absence
of the ego.
                    The Wellsprings

God loves life
in its failure
as much as
in its fruitfulness.
                    The Kingdom

The lover
creates
his beloved,
the Master
his disciple.
                    The Creator

I am fortunate indeed!
I have been granted
the wealth
of another day of life.
                    The Mendicant

To become
creative
learn the art
of wasting time.
                    The Vacation

What worse indictment
than to be spoken well of
by everyone
and to have no enemies?
                    The King

Listen
to the song
the angels sang
when you were born.
                    The Advent

Eternal life
is
here.
Eternal life
is
now.
          The Redemption

Solitude
is
togetherness.
        The Reunion

Wonder
is
the heart
of
contemplation.
        The Discovery

All
people
carry
in them
thoughts
that have the power
to bring them
instant peace.
        The Center

This truth
I firmly hold,
all evidence
to the contrary
notwithstanding:
my life has been
a gift,
a blessing
to the world.
        The Evidence

Does Jesus Christ
have faith
in you?
        The Creator

You will never be
the same
again
from having been
exposed
to the rigors
of aloneness.
        The Desert

For instant peace of mind
return to earth
in fantasy
a thousand years from now
to search
for what remains
of your existence.
        The Deliverance

Where
Jesus
is
dissensions
must
arise.
        The Pioneer

One moment's
acceptance
of everything that is
is better
than a thousand years
of piety.
        The Awakening

I barely know
what will happen
in the future
—but I have seen
its beauty
and its meaning.
> The Evidence

You are made
whole
again
in
silence.
> The Wellsprings

What is the last thing
you desire to see
before you close your eyes
in death?
> The Discovery

I would not be
what I am today
if I had never seen
the sunrise
or the moon
or flowers in bloom
or people's faces.
> The Discovery

Life
is not a problem
to be solved,
a question
to be answered.

Life is a mystery
to be contemplated,
wondered at,
and savored.
> The Symphony

His words
are
an essential part
of the eating
of that bread.
> The Promise

Stop
to think
where
he is calling
when you hear him say,
"Come."
> The Offer

Cite
one experience
that alone
would justify
your life.
> The Essence

Doubt
is faith's friend.
The enemy
of faith
is
fear.
                    The Creator

Nature
—so fragile,
insecure,
exposed to death—
is so alive!
                    The Exposure

The body
on the cross
is a parable
of conquest,
not defeat.
It calls
for envy,
not commiseration.
                    The King

See an event
fully unfold
and you will see
salvation history.
                    The Bible

Contemplate
the impact
of a single drop
of rain
—and you will know
the impact
of your life
on human history.
                    The Comedy

You only live
when you find
a treasure
you would
gladly
die for.
                    The Find

Happiness is not tomorrow.
Happiness is now.
                    The Redemption

I cannot
but resent you,
love divine,
when I feel
you are possessive.
                    The Encounter

To be
alive
and
free
you must shed
your fear
of walking
unaccompanied.
        The Pilgrim

Reality
is
your home—
find it
and you will never more
be lonely.
                    The Pilgrim

The Christ
can say
of me:
"This
is
my
body."
                    The Vessel

If your God
comes to your rescue
and gets you out of trouble
it is time
you started looking
for the true God.
                    The King

Your inner beauty
is reserved
for God's eyes only.
                    The Find

Here is the source
of every human suffering:
to see as permanent
what is,
in essence,
passing.
                    The River

The devotee
must never fear
to "fight" the Lord.
                    The Encounter

I get nowhere
because I fear
to walk
alone.
                    The Pilgrim

I am rich enough
if I can hear
the sound of music
and the song of birds
and human voices.
                    The Awakening

You do not
have
to change
for God
to love
you.
                The Revelation

Having closed
our eyes
we say
he is invisible.
                    The Bible

Be grateful
for your sins.
They are carriers
of grace.
                    The Good News

Say goodbye
to golden yesterdays
—or your heart
will never learn
to love
the present.
                    The Absolute

Count
the blessings
your handicap
has brought
—and you will see
its loneliness.
                    The Awakening

Worship
in the temple
of the present
moment.
                    The Absolute

What
does he see
in me
that
even though he knows
my sinfulness,
he says,
"You are precious
to my heart"?
                    The Darkness

How grateful
you would be
to anyone
who did for you
what you have done
for God!
                    The Good News

You are involved,
immersed
—make sure
you are not drowning.
                    The River

If you
are still
afraid
you have not heard
the good news.
                    The Revolution

Find the cave
within your heart
and you find
everything.
                    The Center

I did not know
that the sun,
the moon,
the evening star
were the words
with which he spoke
to me,
so I never heard
their song,
their cry,
their cosmic silence.
                    The Bible

Solitude
shatters
the illusion
that you
and I
are separate.
                    The Reunion

I am
no great improvement
on the men
who killed
the Savior.
                    The Darkness

You are
responsible
for the offenses
you have been
the victim of.
                    The Redemption

I am
a treasure.

Some day
some where
some one
discovered
me.
                    The Find

God knows
I had no right
to a single hour of life
—or a single hour of you.
                    The Mendicant

Solitude
revives
the gift
of laughter.
                    The Comedy

What song
will you want
your heart
to sing
when you are dying?
                    The Wellsprings

When you are brought
to silence
this book
will be your enemy.
Get rid of it.

Seek
to hold
and not to cling,
enjoy
and not possess.
                    The Nomad

Repentance
reaches
fullness
when you are brought
to gratitude
for your sins.
                    The Redemption

The final power
is to be
at home
with powerlessness.
                    The King

Listen
to the song
in your heart.
                    The Morning

Actions
can be
good or bad.
People
only good.
                    The Education

×

Solitude
is
an act
of love,
a kindness
to myself.
The Mirage

Tell him
what it means
to you
to call him
Lord.

Feel creation throb
to the rhythm
of your heartbeat.

Who
can claim
the credit
of having taught you
how to love?

Can Jesus Christ?

Is your love
of God
secure enough
that you can rage
against him?

Victory
is given
to the one
who dares
to be alone.

The God
who deals in terror
is a bully,
and to bend the knee
before him
is to be a coward,
not a devotee.

You seek
rebirth
—and shun
the unfamiliar?

Dare
to face reality
and say
of everything you cling to:
"This too
will pass away."

Nature is a prolongation
of myself,
my wider body.

List
each revelation
he has made
to you
in friendship.
                    The Recognition

Blind people
come to see
things
that they missed
when they had sight.
                    The Discovery

How does one fear
the Lord
if love
is unconditional?
                    The Encounter

History's
worst atrocities
were carried out
in good faith.
                    The Darkness

Other places
other persons
call to me—
and I must go.
                    The Expedition

In solitude
I have the depth
to see
—and love—
creation.
                    The Reunion

Is
your God
aware
that love
is never
jealous?
                    (1 Cor. 13:5)
                    The Encounter

Darkness
shows
the burning beauty
of the flame.
The thought of death
reveals
life's
fragile
loveliness.
                    The Symphony

How many
of the loves
and dreams
and fears
of yesteryears
retain their hold
on you
today?
                    The River

232

Nothing
has changed
except
my attitude
—so everything
has changed.
                    The Enlightenment

Resentment
turns
to gratitude
when I see
that your offense
has brought me grace.
                    The Redemption

Suspect
the image
you have formed
of God
—it will
please him more
than adoration.
                    The Encounter

Love
keeps no record
of wrongs.
                    (1 Cor. 13:5)

And God
is love.
                    The Good News

You come alive
each time
you dare
to die—
let go,
move on,
bid things goodbye.
                    The Expedition

If you find
your rest
in Jesus Christ
you will never
know
a moment's ease
again.
                    The Offer

Avoid
looking
at yourself
and you successfully
avoid
reality.
                    The Desert

As you flow by
eternally,
I sit
and look
and wonder.
                    The Stream

In solitude
your
self
is given back
to you.
                    The Wellsprings

God
cannot
be seen.
He can be
recognized.
                    The Stranger

Life
is
for
the
gambler.

The Exposure

I know not
what
it calls me to
but I recognize
the voice.
                    The Venture

I fear
to love
so I fear
to be alone.
                    The Reunion

No human being
can reach you
where it really matters.
                    The Desert

When you can freely give
your hands
and feet
for nailing
and your heart
to be pierced
and bled,
you will know
the taste,
at last,
of life
and liberation.
                    The King

No one
can be
grateful
and
unhappy.
                    The Secret

You are severed
from
your
self
and from
reality
by the noise
we call the ego.
When ego disappears
you are made
whole
again
—and silent.
                    The Wellsprings

We stand apart—
only to be sucked
into the stream of life
and flow away.
                    The Rain

Contemplate
life's
essence:

from dance
to dust
to dance.
                    The Symphony

You are made
whole again
in
silence.
                    The Wellsprings

Your center
is
the center
of
the universe.
                    The Heart

Certainty
is
the sin
of bigots,
terrorists,
and Pharisees.
Compassion
makes us think
we may be wrong.
                    The Darkness

I remember
with emotion
the times
I fought his love
—in vain,
for love
is irresistible.
                    The Satellite

My body feels
his touch of burning fire
—and tender playfulness.
                    The Touch

Come, take my eyes
to see your own creation
and my ears to hear
the melodies you compose.
                    The Symphony

Peace
is only found
in yes.
                    The Surrender

In every word
I say,
each action
I perform,
God intervenes
in human history.
                    The Bible

Listen
to the good news:
God is unjust—
he makes the sun
to shine
on the good
and bad
alike.
                    The Revolution

I stand
before him
speechless,
wonder-struck,
uncomprehending.
                    The Ecstasy

Come home
and the self will soon
be silent
and God will be revealed.
                    The Return

Sink
into your roots
in nature
and
you will find
yourself.
                    The Wellsprings

The sea
absorbs impurities,
remaining undefiled.
                    The Ocean

Solitude
restores
reality.
                    The Vacation

The Messiah's
still
around.
When
did you see
him
last?
                    The Stranger

Would
you be any
different
if
Jesus Christ
did not exist?
                    The Lord

On the day
you cease
to change
you cease
to live.
                    The Exposure

You sanctify
whatever
you are grateful for.
The Advent

Listen
to the wordless wisdom
of the flame.
The Flame

How rich
are Nature's songs,
how deep her silence!
The Morning

A thousand seeds
must perish
for every flower that blooms.
The Kingdom

No evil can withstand
the sunshine
of awareness.
The Day

Conflict
is
the royal road
to union.
The Encounter

Extend
your arms
in welcome
to the future.
The best
is yet to come!
The Expedition

I am one
of the countless
particles
of dust
that dance
in the rays
of the universal sun.
The Heart

Renounce nothing.
Cling to nothing.
The Nomad

Mysticism
is
felt gratitude
for
everything.
The Awakening

Only
look
—and
someday
you
will
see.
            The Water